OPPORTU

in

Marine Science and Maritime Careers

HILLSBORO PUBLIC LIBRARIES
Hillsboro, OR
Member of Washington County
COOPERATIVE LIBRARY SERVICES

OPPORTUNITIES

in

Marine Science and Maritime Careers

REVISED EDITION

RAY HEITZMANN

HILLSBORO PUBLIC LIBRARIES
Hillsboro, OR
Member of Washington County
COOPERATIVE LIBRARY SERVICES

McGraw·Hill

New York   Chicago   San Francisco   Lisbon   London   Madrid   Mexico City
Milan   New Delhi   San Juan   Seoul   Singapore   Sydney   Toronto

The *McGraw-Hill* Companies

Library of Congress Cataloging-in-Publication Data

Heitzmann, Ray.
    Opportunities in marine science and maritime careers / by Ray Heitzmann. —
Rev. ed.
        p.   cm.
    Rev. ed. of: Opportunities in marine and maritime careers / Wm. Ray Heitzmann ;
foreword by Jean-Michel Cousteau. c1988.
      ISBN 0-07-144851-9 (alk. paper)
      1. Merchant marine—Vocational guidance—United States.   2. Naval art and
science—Vocational guidance—United States.   3. Oceanography—Vocational
guidance—United States.   4. Fisheries—Vocational guidance—United States.
I. Heitzmann, Ray. Opportunities in marine and maritime careers.   II. Title.

VK160.H37   2006
387.5'023'73—dc22   2005020281

Copyright © 2006 by The McGraw-Hill Companies, Inc. All rights reserved. Printed in the
United States of America. Except as permitted under the United States Copyright Act of
1976, no part of this publication may be reproduced or distributed in any form or by any
means, or stored in a database or retrieval system, without the prior written permission of
the publisher.

1 2 3 4 5 6 7 8 9 0 DOC/DOC 0 9 8 7 6

ISBN 0-07-144851-9
3291 7406 4/06
Interior design by Rattray Design

McGraw-Hill books are available at special quantity discounts to use as premiums and
sales promotions, or for use in corporate training programs. For more information, please
write to the Director of Special Sales, Professional Publishing, McGraw-Hill, Two Penn
Plaza, New York, NY 10121-2298. Or contact your local bookstore.

This book is printed on acid-free paper.

To my family: past, present, and future.
And to the marine/maritime family everywhere.

CONTENTS

Foreword   xi
Preface   xiii
Acknowledgments   xvii
Introduction   xxi

1. **Aquaria-Related Careers**   1

Typical careers. Aquaria and oceanaria.

2. **Cruise Ship Careers**   17

Requirements. Careers. Getting started. Ship lines.

3. **Oceanography and the Marine Sciences** 31

Typical careers. Requirements. Job outlook. Sea Grant
programs.

4. **Fishing**   49

Educators. Administrators. Researchers. Management positions. Aquaculture positions. Job outlook. Sources of additional information.

5. **Commercial Diving**   61

Specific jobs. Undersea submersible diving. Schools.

6. **Maritime Transportation**   73

Portside opportunities. Ships and shipping. Oceangoing opportunities. Education and training. Oceangoing working conditions. Merchant marine officers. Inland maritime careers. Developing your skills.

7. **Shipbuilding**   101

Naval architects. Marine engineers. Skilled crafts.

8. **Military Careers Afloat**   115

United States Navy. Enlisted personnel. The naval officer. United States Coast Guard.

9. **Miscellaneous Marine Science and Maritime Careers**   137

Marine technicians. Nautical archaeologists. Ship restorers. Maritime museum careers. Pilots. Women afloat. Admiralty law. Bait and fishing shop owners

and employees. Baitfish catchers. Marine insurance
careers. Seafood processing and marketing careers.
Academic careers.

10. Getting Your Feet Wet   **163**

Precareer experiences. Sea Cadets. Sea Explorers.
Naval Junior Reserve Officers Training Corps. The
Girl Scouts.

Appendix: Maritime Museums   177
Recommended Reading   189

FOREWORD

TOGETHER WITH MY father, Jacques Cousteau, I have been a witness, often firsthand, to humankind's entry into the sea as never before—on scuba as men-fish in small maneuverable submarines, and as aquanauts living day after day in the liquid world without sun. As we have entered the ocean in greater numbers and in more diverse ways, we have learned much not only about the sea but about ourselves as well.

As a young architect, my dream was to design underwater cities. I realize now this will only come to pass as an exotic oddity or as an occasional underwater hotel or science research station because, even with the wonders of our technology, we are still aliens under the sea; we are able to visit in ecstatic excursions, but we are unable to settle.

Though the sea has taught us of our limitations, it has also expanded our vision, as we watch through film the many forms life has taken and the ways in which fish and worm and whale have evolved to survive. The study of a coral reef is a description of a large city in which competing and cooperating races and professionals and individuals live and thrive and die. It is a balance that allows the reef to continue for thousands and thousands of relatively undisturbed years. Much of what we have learned at sea is a parable of what we could do on land.

But watching, smelling, feeling, tasting, and thinking about the sea did more than teach me—it changed me forever into a man in love with the sea, just as my father was and his father before him. We quickly learned that people protect what they love, and we are in love with the sea.

In reading this informative book and considering whether you want an ocean career, you will find you have many choices; some of them will exhilarate you and some will disappoint you. Choose wisely and base your decision on what you love. Few go to sea to become rich; however, almost no one comes back from the sea who isn't enriched as a human being. Be practical about your choices and spend all the time you can on every rocking boat, mudflat, or laboratory. See for yourself how the sea suits you. Then love her with passion and save her through your work.

Jean-Michel Cousteau
Director, Jean-Michel Institute
Santa Barbara, California

PREFACE

WHEN THE FIRST edition of this book was written more than twenty-five years ago, there existed a great need to remind citizens of the United States of America of their rich maritime traditions and the vitally important role water played in their lives. That need still exists. In fact, our neighbors to the north seem more in touch with the marine world than we do.

Although boarded by eleven thousand miles of coastline, many Americans behave as if the United States is a landlocked nation. The marine science and maritime enterprise has become so ingrained in our traditions that we rarely give it much thought. For example, much of our language comes from nautical terms: words like *first-rate, shipshape, blubber, ironclad, the whole nine yards,* and *windfall* demonstrate how sea terms have entered into land use. Our economy, architecture, religion, music, and literature all bear the stamp of the sea.

This planet, of which approximately 75 percent is covered by water, has been well served by the sea. Early societies lived near rivers, on islands, or along oceans from which they obtained food, transportation, and trade—in a word, survival.

Over the last several decades, we Americans have slowly begun to realize our debt to our rivers, lakes, and seas and our obligation to preserve them. Stories in newspapers and books, shows on television—some featuring Jacques Cousteau—the work of schoolteachers in presenting the marine curriculum, the wonderful contribution of the aquaria and oceanaria, the "tall ship" spectaculars, and the maritime industry's public crusade have helped to remind people of our nautical traditions. Given our heritage and this book's emphasis on careers, it is useful to recall the words of Margaret Widdemer in her poem "Sea Call."

> My old love for the water has come back again—
> I had forgotten its surging, so long, so long away;
> Sapphire-blue in the sunlight and green-gray in the rain,
> And the same waves cresting, and the same sharp spray.
>
> There was left a wave in my heart when I went to the inland
>   towns,
> Something that moved and murmured in the days when I
>   forgot;
> Vivid flowers of the gardens or thick long grass of the downs
> What were the sweets of the summer days, where the calling
>   waves were not?
>
> My old love for the water has come back once more;
> The wave of the deep draws full, and the wave in my heart lifts
>   high;
> This is my own old country and my own old shore . . .
> And I cannot leave the water till the day I die.

There exists great interdependence within the marine science and maritime communities. For example, those in commercial fishing work with marine biologists, those in maritime transportation rely on harbor pilots, and naval personnel often collaborate on research with oceanographers studying chemical aspects of the seas. Consequently, I strongly suggest that you read this book in its entirety, as opposed to reading a couple chapters, because of the interconnectedness of the world of water.

Acknowledgments

The COMPREHENSIVE NATURE of a book on marine and maritime careers requires the cooperation of a number of individuals and organizations. The following deserve special mention.

Ms. Regina Agrusa, Director, Pupil Personnel Services, Sewanhaka School District, Floral Park, New York; Ms. Andrea Green Bry, Ocean View, New Jersey; Ms. Teresa Wojcik, The University of Pennsylvania; Ms. Kelly Green Yoh, The Haverford School, Pennsylvania; Ms. Nora Deans, Director, Publications, Monterey Bay Aquarium, California; Ms. Margaret Buchholz; publisher, editor, author Harvey Cedars, New Jersey; Ms. Joy Wolf, Director, Education Department, Sea World of California; Ms. Susan Alpert and Ms. Carolyn Stone, Public Relations, Cunard Line; Mr. David D. Beach, Manager, Technical Services, National Marine Manufacturers Association; Mr. Thomas V. MacEwen, Vice President, Prudential Lines; Mr. Walter Oates, Public Affairs Officer, Merchant Marine Administration, Washington DC; Dr. Chris Harrison, Dean, Rosenthal School of Marine and Atmospheric Science,

University of Miami; Ms. Gretchen Waterbury, Chapman School of Seamanship, Stuart, Florida; Mr. Rick Tinnin, Marine Science Institute, University of Texas; Mr. Jeffrey A. Smith, Vice President, Public Affairs, The American Waterways Operators Inc.; Mr. Les Bartholow, Office of Maritime Labor and Training, United States Department of Transportation; Mr. Enno Reckendorf, Director, The Norfolk School of Building; Ms. Nancy Richardson, Girl Scouts of the United States of America; Hon. Curt Weldon, U.S. House of Representatives (Pennsylvania); Dr. James Merrill, Maritime Historian (Emeritus), University of Delaware; Ms. Mary Heitzmann Kingwill, Media/Technology Specialist, Weehawken Schools, New Jersey; Ms. Sharon Meeker, Sea Grant, University of New Hampshire; Claire Antonucci, Director of Education, New Jersey Marine Sciences Consortium; Dr. Nicole Crane, Monterey Peninsula College (California); Dru Clarke, Kansas State University; Tracey Szmajda and Sonya Litwack, Villanova University, Pennsylvania; Dr. Lundie Spence, Sea Grant, North Carolina State University/University of North Carolina; Mr. F. A. Courtenay Jr., National President, the Propeller Club of the United States, Portland, Oregon; G. Linda Crisculo, Washington Township High School, New Jersey; Mr. K. T. Weaver, Executive Director, United States Naval Sea Cadet Corps; Dr. Val Chase, Biologist, The National Aquarium, Baltimore; Professor Ken Stibolt, Anne Arundel Community College, Arnold, Maryland; Glenn S. Gordiner, Research Associate, Mystic Seaport Museum, Connecticut; Dr. Bill Hall, Marine Education Specialist, the College of Marine Studies, University of Delaware; Mr. Bill Ward, Education Director, Independence Seaport Museum, Philadelphia; Mr. Rod Koon, Director of Port Relations, Port of Tacoma, Washington; Mr. John Wiegman, Assistant Director, and Major Ken Conklin, Vice President, Seafarers Harry Lundeberg School of Seamanship, Piney Point, Maryland; Mr. Robert E. Banks, Director of Marketing, South Jersey Port Corporation; Mr. Arthur W. Kane, Vice President, Corporate Relations, Norwegian Caribbean Lines; Ms. Krista Trono, Communication Coordinator, *Monitor*, National Marine Sanctuary; Ms. Liz Love, Monterey Bay National Marine Sanctuary, California; Mr. James A. Barber Jr., Executive Director, United States Navy Institute; Mr. Peter Stanford, Editor-Publisher, *Sea History*; Ms. Bonnie Bekken, Social Studies School Service, Los Angeles; Lt. Matt Zurcher, NROTC, Villanova University; Mr. Thomas Greene, Oceanography Department, Kingsborough Community College, Brooklyn, New York; Kevin Walsh, Anchor, CN8 Comcast Television; Eileen Wilkinston, St. Mark's High School, Newark, Delaware; Professors Landry, Davis, Seitz, and Wilkie of Texas A & M University at Galveston; Robert Fraunberger, Bryn Mawr, Pennsylvania; Wil Tolen, Tolen Marine, Paducah, Kentucky; Ms. Lee Stack, Villanova University; Mary Heitzmann Focht, Clifton Park, New York; Rick Heitzmann, New York; and Gardner T. Heitzmann.

INTRODUCTION

THE WORLD OF water offers an incredible number of exciting and rewarding careers that make an important contribution to our society. People in these jobs draw satisfaction not only from the personal enjoyment of their tasks, but also from the fact that they are helping others. Consider the following possibilities.

• You have enhanced the quality of numerous urban locations through positive waterfront development. Your next challenge is convincing all parties that Weehawken, New Jersey, located on the Hudson River directly opposite New York City, can become the nation's premier waterfront locale. Your background in urban architecture and marine studies makes you a perfect fit for this demanding task.

• You're a scientist and your current specialty has you investigating shipworms. These critters regularly devastate wooden vessels, piers, and pilings, costing millions. Your research has made an important contribution to controlling this "termite of the sea."

• You have studied underwater archaeology, and now you and your team have located and explored a shipwreck off the coast of Texas in the Gulf of Mexico. The expedition has brought to the surface artifacts that will provide insights to the historical era during which the ship operated. You have spent many months examining historical documents and old maps, securing government permission, and arranging for the latest technology to aid your search, and it has paid off.

• Here they come! You're entering your tenth year as a marine education specialist, and today you will be taking a group of sophomores from a local high school out on the Delaware Bay. First the students will be given a lecture on safety afloat and then some information about the bay. The students plan to take water samples and conduct some experiments back at school. You know it will be a very long day, but you also realize that the kids will love it and leave with a better understanding, appreciation, and respect for the marine environment.

• Your ship floats across the ocean as you stand on the deck, the wind blowing in your face. The freighter carries a cargo of heavy agricultural machinery to the west coast of Africa, where upon docking you will spend a few days before returning with a cargo of materials for American industry.

• Mayday! Mayday! Your Barnegat Light Coast Guard station in New Jersey has just received an SOS distress call, and you have been ordered to rescue a sinking twenty-two-foot pleasure boat. Those aboard the small craft were enjoying a lovely Sunday afternoon cruise when a sudden, serious storm hit, imperiling their lives. Aided by your speeding boat and equipment, you arrive in time and successfully rescue the boaters. As you return to shore and receive the praise of your supervisor and the thanks of those whom you've saved from a watery death, you feel proud of your chosen profession.

• Aquaculture (fish farming) has had great success and promises an even greater future. It's clearly one of the most exciting projects in New Jersey's cities in years, and you're the marine science advisor. The plan is to raise fish in deserted factories and warehouses. Once the fish reach marketable size, they will be shipped to fish markets on the East Coast. This aspect of aquaculture has great potential.

• The beaches in your state have suffered badly from what the media call the "El Niño" effect. The governor has asked you to provide technical skills in a project that will replenish the beaches and prevent future problems to the coastline.

• Your life as a marine biologist has led you to California. You are studying the growth of giant kelp at a test farm located about five miles off the coast of Corona del Mar. The test farm is anchored in five hundred feet of water. The brown seaweed grows in water depths of only one hundred feet or fewer because of its need for sunlight. Upon harvesting, the experimental kelp will produce gas through a special process, thus in part alleviating the world's reliance on oil. You enjoy the excitement of your work and your potential contribution to the well-being of not only the nation, but of the world as well.

• One of the fish species living in the streams of your state has contracted a disease. Because of the fear that the disease will spread, you and your supervisor, a fish culturalist, have traveled around the state examining fish. Specifically, in your capacity as assistant, you have taken blood samples and analyzed them to see if the disease has spread to fish in other ponds or streams of the state. Each day you arrive back at your motel room tired but happy with your chosen job.

• While pursuing community college courses in marine propulsion technology, you work part-time in a local marina. Because of the scarcity of trained people, you can work as much as you wish. However, your laboratory courses (particularly Marine Ignition and Fuel Systems) consume much of your time. At the end of two years, you will receive your associate in science degree. From several job offers, you've narrowed your choice to two—assistant marina manager or marine diesel technician for a local fishing fleet. Not only does your future look financially sound, you will have the satisfaction of living and working near the water.

• The great interest in the world of water has created a hunger for information on maritime and marine science topics. You have always enjoyed writing. Now you write a syndicated monthly column entitled "Nautically Notable: The World of Water" for the general public. A series of television programs and radio spots loom as possibilities.

• Fish farming in Idaho? Yes! In Buhl, Idaho, a company is developing a fish without bones. Believe it or not, millions of pounds of fish a year are raised through aquaculture. The Idaho project, of which you are the director, shows outstanding promise.

Do the above scenarios seem intriguing, challenging, and in tune with your career interests? If so, please read on to find the strategies you can pursue to achieve job satisfaction in a marine or maritime career. Just as with other occupations, people in marine and maritime careers spend many hours a day in routine detail work that is necessary for the success of any task. For this reason, many employers want people with specific marine or maritime abilities combined with good habits such as punctuality, writing and speaking skills, and a strong work ethic.

This book provides information on several marine and maritime careers. You are strongly encouraged to write to and/or check websites for additional information on jobs that appear interesting. Many sources of information are cited in the text and in the Appendix and Recommended Reading sections in the back of the book. The schools mentioned herein are used as examples; discussion of them does not constitute an endorsement.

AQUARIA-RELATED CAREERS

THERE EXISTS A virtual "aquarium frenzy" in North America; aquariums are clearly one of the most attention-getting facilities of which a city can boast. Not only do they entertain visitors, but they also serve a vital educational function and, for our purposes, house many exotic and fun careers. Consider what Gretchen Crapa has to say about her position: "My job is varied. I enjoy the opportunity to interact with visitors of all ages and interests." Gretchen works at the National Aquarium in Baltimore (www.aqua.org). Throughout a typical year, she engages in a variety of interesting activities, such as the following:

- Teach student, member, and general public programs
- Develop and write lessons
- Coordinate workshops for teachers
- Organize special events
- Train and supervise summer employees and interns
- Work on the aquarium's Web page

- Plan and lead trips to various locations (Florida keys or Massachusetts coast, for example)
- Attend conferences

Gretchen believes she has one of the most desirable jobs in the world of water. "I have always felt a deep affinity for the ocean and have been interested in marine creatures since I was a child. I have wonderful memories of spending hours at the touch pool at the Roanoke Aquarium." Undoubtedly, Gretchen was one of those visitors who asked, "How can I get a job at an aquarium?" This is one of the most frequently asked questions in the marine world today.

Typical Careers

Several types of jobs exist at aquaria: some people work with animals, some with the public, some with both, and still others perform completely different jobs.

Gretchen began her career in the middle of a desert! While attending college at the University of Arizona (Sonoran Desert), she discovered "marine education" through a program that brought live animals, slides, and artifacts from the Sea of Cortez to schools in and around Tucson, Arizona. Observing the excited faces of the children prompted her to continue to explore the marine world. After a summer internship at the Monterey Bay Aquarium, she became fully committed to her career. Although currently employed in the education department of the National Aquarium, she continues to grow by pursuing a master's degree in environmental science and policy.

A variety of positions exist at most aquaria. Many workers are employed behind the scenes and rarely work with animals or have contact with visitors. For example, plumbers, artists, engineers, housekeepers, electricians, accountants, and others all contribute to the success of the facility. Some of the careers more directly related to marine life at the National Aquarium in Baltimore (as well as other aquaria) are described in the following paragraphs.

Aquarists maintain all aspects of the aquatic exhibits; this includes maintaining water quality, feeding the fish, cleaning the tanks, and completing related tasks such as precise record keeping. People in these positions have backgrounds in marine or aquatic science, as well as SCUBA (Self-Contained Underwater Breathing Apparatus) certification.

Aviculturists work with the marine birds and maintain all aspects of the display. This aquarium is unique in possessing such an exhibit. People employed in this specialty have a background in biology or zoology and have excellent public speaking skills.

Marine educators give presentations to visitors and teach classes. This requires an excellent knowledge of the various fish and birds, good speaking skills, and the ability to work with children. These individuals have backgrounds in science, usually marine science or biology.

Herpetologists manage the reptile and amphibian collection. They feed and care for these species. Again, a background in the biological sciences is a must, as well as close attention to detail. As with all animals at the aquarium, this collection must be carefully observed to maintain optimum health.

Many other specialties remain critical to the success of an aquarium: *veterinarians* and their assistants—*veterinary technicians*—oversee the health of the animals. Veterinarians hold a medical degree (D.V.M.) in animal medicine; veterinary technicians graduate from two- or four-year colleges and pass licensing examinations. Water-quality technicians ensure the quality and safety of the water environment.

Marine mammal trainers are perhaps the most popular and sought-after of the aquaria-related careers. Armed with a background in psychology and/or biology, fine public speaking skills, and SCUBA certification, marine mammal trainers work with dolphins, seals, and orcas (killer whales). Though often visible as part of the "shows," these individuals labor many hours behind the scenes in training activities. They also help to maintain the tanks and the exhibit area. If this sounds a little like show business, perhaps it is.

Consider the career of Julie Scardina, *animal ambassador* and *curator of animal training* at Sea World of California (www.sea world.com). A weekly contributor to "Jack Hanna's Animal Adventures" and recent guest on "The Tonight Show" with Jay Leno, "Live with Regis and Kelly," and other programs, she has not only the skills but also the confidence to appear on television before millions of people. In preparation for training and performing with the eight-thousand-pound Shamu, sea lions, otters, and walruses, she obtained her college degree from San Diego State University with a major in psychology and a minor in biology and then earned an associate's degree in exotic animal training and management from Moorpath College in California. Her career permits her to interact with some of the world's most fascinating teachers and to provide education to children and adults. Clearly this occupation offers personal benefits as well as contributions to our society. For more information contact:

International Marine Animal Trainers' Association
John G. Shedd Aquarium
1200 South Lake Shore Drive
Chicago, IL 60605
www.imata.org

Marine mammal scientists work closely with marine mammals; although some work at aquaria, most work in other environments. Employed by organizations ranging from marine laboratories to the U.S. Navy to the fishing industry, they study the behavior of a wide variety of marine animals. Despite the allure of this career, opportunities remain limited. Consequently, a strong background in science with very good grades are a must. Many have gained experience while serving as volunteers at aquaria or as interns with private companies or government organizations. Most have graduate degrees and specialize; that is, they confine their study to a particular marine mammal—dolphin, manatee, and so forth. The following website contains additional information: www.une.edu.

Some colleges have begun to offer specific programs, training, and courses for those interested in the field. Located in Southern California, Saddleback College (www.saddleback.cc.ca.us) offers a certificate program in Aquarium and Aquaculture Science. Courses such as "Marine Aquarium Systems" and "Management of Marine Aquariums" assist beginning students as well as those already in the field to upgrade their skills and knowledge.

Visiting and volunteering at aquaria or oceanaria can serve as valuable career preparation. Technically, aquaria emphasize marine ecosystems involving all species, including marine mammals. They fall into the following categories: publicly owned or governmentally owned, not for profit, and privately owned for profit. Oceanaria, such as Sea World, are privately owned for profit, and they tend to emphasize marine mammals.

Aquaria tend to focus on special exhibits, some of which change periodically. Canada's Vancouver Aquarium has had a "Whale Fest"; Monterey Bay Aquarium had a magnificent "Jellyfish" exhibit; the New York Aquarium (Brooklyn) boasts a "Bermuda Triangle" that emphasizes marine animals (sea turtles, moray eels) from that region; the Aquarium of the Americas in New Orleans has a wonderful Mississippi Delta exhibit; the North Carolina Aquarium at Roanoke Island features a freshwater "Turtle Pond"; and the Maritime Aquarium in Norwalk, Connecticut, integrates the marine and maritime worlds.

Aquaria and Oceanaria

The aquaria and oceanaria listed here offer wonderful opportunities for observing not only the animals but also how their human caretakers interact with and tend to them. They may also provide opportunities for volunteer or paid positions for those interested in working in this environment.

Aquarium of the Americas
1 Canal Street
New Orleans, LA 70130
www.auduboninstitute.org/aoa/index.php

Aquarium of the National Marine Fisheries Service
166 Water Street
Woods Hole, MA 02543-1097
www.whoi.edu

Aquarium of Niagara Falls
701 Whirlpool Street
Niagara Falls, NY 14301
www.aquariumofniagara.org

Aquarium for Wildlife Conservation
Boardwalk and West Eighth Street
Brooklyn, NY 11224
www.nyaquarium.com

Bermuda Aquarium, Museum, and Zoo
P.O. Box FL 145
Flatts FLBX, Bermuda
www.bamz.org

Clearwater Marine Science Center Aquarium
249 Windward Passage
Clearwater, FL 34630
www.cmaquarium.org

Dallas World Aquarium
P.O. Box 150113
Dallas, TX 75315-0113
www.dwazoo.com

John G. Shedd Aquarium
1200 South Lake Shore Drive
Chicago, IL 60605
www.sheddaquarium.org

The Living Seas
P.O. Box 10000
Lake Buena Vista, FL 32830
http://disneyworld.disney.go.com/wdw/parks/attractiondetail?id=the
livingseasnattractionpage

Marine World Africa USA
Marine World Parkway
Vallejo, CA 94589
www.dot.ca.gov/hq/rail/depots/stops/vmw.htm

Marineland of Florida
9507 Ocean Shore Boulevard
Marineland, FL 32086
www.marineland.net

The Maritime Center at Norwalk
10 North Water Street
Norwalk, CT 06854
www.maritimeaquarium.org

Miami Seaquarium
4400 Rickenbaker Causeway
Miami, FL 33149
www.miamiseaquarium.com/index.htm

Monterey Bay Aquarium
886 Cannery Row
Monterey, CA 93940-1085
www.mbayaq.org

Mount Desert Oceanarium
172 Clark Road
Southwest Harbor, ME 04679
www.theoceanarium.com

Mystic Marinelife Aquarium
55 Coogan Boulevard
Mystic, CT 06355-1997
www.mysticaquarium.org

National Aquarium
U.S. Department of Commerce Building
Fourteenth and Constitution Avenue NW
Washington, DC 20230
www.nationalaquarium.com

National Aquarium in Baltimore
Pier 3, 501 East Pratt Street
Baltimore, MD 21202-3194
www.aqua.org

New England Aquarium
Central Wharf
Boston, MA 02110
www.neaq.org

New Jersey State Aquarium at Camden
1 Riverside Drive
Camden, NJ 08103-1060
www.njaquarium.org

North Carolina Aquarium at Fort Fisher
2201 Fort Fisher Boulevard South, Box 1
Kure Beach, NC 28449
www.ncaquariums.com

North Carolina Aquarium at Pine Knoll Shores
P.O. Box 580
Atlantic Beach, NC 28512-0580
www.ncaquariums.com

North Carolina Aquarium on Roanoke Island
P.O. Box 967
Airport Road
Manteo, NC 27954
www.ncaquariums.com

Oregon Coast Aquarium
2820 Southeast Ferry Slip Road
Newport, OR 97365
www.aquarium.org

Sea Life Park Hawaii
41-202 Kalanianaole Highway, Suite 7
Waimanalo, HI 96795
www.sealifeparkhawaii.com

Sea World of California
1720 South Shores Road
San Diego, CA 92109-7995
www.seaworld.com

Sea World of Florida
7007 Sea World Drive
Orlando, FL 32821-8097
www.seaworld.com

Sea World of Ohio
1100 Sea World Drive
Aurora, OH 44202
www.seaworld.com

Sea World of Texas
10500 Sea World Drive
San Antonio, TX 78251
www.seaworld.com

The Seattle Aquarium
1483 Alaskan Way, Pier 59
Seattle, WA 98101-2059
www.seattleaquarium.org

South Dakota Discovery Center and Aquarium
805 West Sioux Avenue
Pierre, SD 57501
www.sd-discovery.com

Steinhart Aquarium
Golden Gate Park
San Francisco, CA 94118-4599
www.calacademy.org

Stephen Birch Aquarium-Museum
Scripps Institution of Oceanography
University of California–San Diego
La Jolla, CA 92093
www.aquarium.ucsd.edu

Tennessee Aquarium
P.O. Box 11048
Chattanooga, TN 37401-2048
www.tennis.org

The Texas State Aquarium
P.O. Box 331307
Corpus Christi, TX 78463
www.texasstateaquarium.org

University of Puerto Rico
Department of Marine Sciences Museum
P.O. Box 5000
Mayaguez, PR 00681-5000
cima.uprm.edu

Vancouver Aquarium
P.O. Box 3232
Vancouver, British Columbia
Canada V6B 3X8
www.vancouver-aquarium.org

Waikiki Aquarium
2777 Kalakaua Avenue
Honolulu, HI 96815
www.waquarium.org

The following organizations active in the marine world can provide additional information:

American Fisheries Society
5410 Grosvenor Lane, Suite 110
Bethesda, MD 20814
www.fisheries.org

American Society of Mammalogists
Institute of Ecosystem Studies
Box AB
Millbrook, NY 12545

American Society of Mammalogists
Virginia Museum of Natural History
1001 Douglas Avenue
Martinsville, VA 24112
www.mammalsociety.org

Center for Coastal Studies
Box 1036
Provincetown, MA 02657
www.coastalstudies.org

Cetacean Behavior Laboratory
Department of Psychology
San Diego State University
San Diego, CA 92182
www.sci.sdsu.edu/cbl/cblhome.html

Coastal Ecosystems Research Foundation
2173 West Sixth Avenue, #207
Vancouver, British Columbia
Canada V6K 1V5
www.cerf.bc.ca/index.asp

EarthWatch
680 Mount Auburn Street
P.O. Box 403
Watertown, MA 02272-9104
www.earthwatch.org

Kewalo Basin Marine Mammal Laboratory
1129 Ala Moana Boulevard
Honolulu, HI 96814
www.dolphin-institute.org

Marine Mammal Research Group
EPCOT Center Trailer #251
Walt Disney World Company
P.O. Box 10000
Lake Buena Vista, FL 32830-1000
www.gse.mq.edu.au/research/mmrg/index_nn.htm

Marine Mammal Research Program
Texas A&M, University at Galveston
Department of Fisheries and Wildlife
4700 Avenue U, Building 303
Galveston, TX 77551
www.tamug.tamu.edu/mmrp

Marine Science Association
Biology Department, Box 18540
Jackson State University
Jackson, MS 39217
www.marinemammalogy.org/strat.htm

Mingan Island Cetacean Study
285 Green Street
Lambert, Quebec Canada J4P 1T3
www.rorqual.com

National Oceanic and Atmospheric Administration
1335 East-West Highway
Silver Spring, MD 20910
www.noaa.gov

National Wildlife Federation
1400 Sixteenth Street NW
Washington, DC 20036
www.nwf.org

Pacific Whale Foundation
Kealia Beach Plaza
101 North Kihei Road, Suite 21
Kihei, HI 96753-8833
www.pacificwhale.org

Theater of the Sea
P.O. Box 407
Islamorada, FL 33036
www.theaterofthesea.com

U.S. Fish and Wildlife Service
1001 East Tudor Road
Anchorage, AK 99503
www.fws.gov

Whale Research Group
230 Mount Scio Road
Memorial University of Newfoundland
St. John's, Newfoundland
Canada A1C 5S7
www.compusult.nf.ca/ditt/wrg.htm

Wheelock College
Whale Net
200 The River Way
Boston, MA 01982
http://whale.wheelock.edu

Women's Aquatic Network
Box 4993
Washington, DC 20008
www.womensaquatic.net

2

CRUISE SHIP CAREERS

IT'S VERY GLAMOROUS. It's fun. It's demanding. And it's hard work!

The cruise ship industry has experienced dramatic growth with several million passengers currently cruising and revenues in the billions. Many new ships, some of them very large, are under now construction.

Jobs are plentiful and if you enjoy traveling, meeting people, and going to exotic destinations, this may be your dream job. A wide variety of careers exists, and almost every major city in North America can boast of passenger ships ready to depart. A warning: There is little downtime for employees as many demands must be met onboard a cruise ship. Most individuals work for two to four years, have a great time, and then "retire" to employment ashore.

Requirements

Those who wish to work on a passenger ship must have background and experience in a specific job. For example, servers, aerobics instructors, cosmetologists, and wine stewards all must have training and experience on land before ever boarding a ship. Don't despair; some jobs require only low-level skills that can be easily learned. In addition to training and experience, there are a number of other important requirements, starting with excellent health. Most ships will have a medical doctor onboard to assist guests and crew in case of emergency. However, the medical care is minimal, and employers don't want personnel who have frequent illnesses resulting from the demands of work aboard ship.

Although age is generally not a factor, people in their twenties and thirties have an edge; nonetheless, a demand does exist for those in their forties, fifties, and even in their sixties for specific jobs. For example, perhaps the most unique career aboard ship is that of the "Gentleman Host." These individuals must be "refined social dancers" between the ages of forty-five and seventy-two who "enjoy enriching the lives of others." For more information visit www.theworkingvacation.com.

The ability to speak a foreign language will increase the probability of obtaining a job; many non-English-speaking tourists are on ships, and a foreign language will help you in your job search on foreign vessels.

Two personality traits are extremely important to success aboard ship—flexibility and dependability. Flexibility is important because a person's lifestyle will change drastically. Dependability is equally important. Although life aboard ship appears glamorous—it is for the guests—it is not necessarily glamorous for the staff. Too often those who labored to obtain a cruise ship job quit after a few months; approximately 25 percent of first-time employees do not fulfill their contractual commitment (usually one or two years). Thus, reliability ranks as an important personal characteristic.

Careers

Aboard ship two categories of careers exist: those that deal with the ship, and those that are related to the cruise-hotel aspect of the pleasure vessel.

The cruise ship has officers and a crew concerned with its navigation, maintenance, propulsion, and so on. This would be comparable to any maritime vessel (see Chapter 6). The routes to these jobs would be through the merchant marine academies and the training programs of the various unions. Also, former naval officers and crew may land positions in these areas.

The following paragraphs describe some of the jobs related to the luxury hotel–cruise type careers. All of these careers require the ability to relate well to people, and to assist guests and make sure they have a good time.

Bartenders prepare drinks at the various bars located throughout the ship. Experience is a must, as are knowledge of the current "in" drink, the score and details of the previous night's game, the developments on television reality shows, and the latest gossip surrounding Hollywood celebrities.

Cosmetologists and *barbers* perform the hairdressing necessities for the passengers. Normally these individuals have excellent styling skills and often have reputations in their field; they also possess wonderful conversational skills.

Cruise directors supervise the staff to maximize the enjoyment of the passengers. For example, a director will arrange for tours when the ship docks at the various ports during the cruise. It is often the director who handles most of the problems that arise for passengers. Persons wishing a position as cruise director would list extensive travel experience and tenure as an assistant director. Often the success of the cruise is directly related to the competence of the director.

Ship's photographers offer passengers the opportunity to remember their voyage through photographs. This busy position (some larger ships will have two or more photographers) requires travel ashore and attendance at parties and special events. Skills involved in this position are those required of any quality professional photographer. If you would like to inquire about this career, contact the following:

TransOcean Photos
New York Cruise Ship Terminal, Suite A
West Fifty-Fourth Street and Twelfth Avenue
New York, NY 10019

Sales personnel aboard ship work in places such as the gift shop. This is often a concession on a ship, so those seeking employment must apply to the appropriate concession company. Obviously retail experience is necessary for this job.

Wine stewards are the wine experts aboard ship. They answer passengers' questions concerning the best wine to drink with certain foods and the correct procedures related to wine drinking. Often these individuals have attended specific schools to obtain their expertise.

Chief pursers, as may be gathered from the name, handle many of the financial aspects of the cruise. For example, a purser handles the crew's payroll. This person also serves as the manager of the cruise personnel. The cruise director reports to the chief purser. Extensive leadership ability and financial experience are prerequisites for this position.

Numerous other cruise ship careers exist. They include:

Assistant cruise directors
Athletic/sports directors
Casino workers of all varieties
Chefs
Dancers
Dining room captains
Dining room servers
Fitness directors
Lecturers
Masseuses/masseurs
Medical doctors
Musicians
Nurses
Social directors
Stewards
Youth activities coordinators

If this sounds like a lot of people work aboard a ship, you're correct. Typical is the *Song of America*, an average-sized ship. It sails out of the Port of Miami with a crew of more than five hundred!

Getting Started

If a career on the high seas sounds a little too exciting, consider working for a passenger ship that cruises the inland waters or the waters along the coast. A number of opportunities exist in this area. The *Scotia Prince* operates out of Portland, Maine, and sails to Nova Scotia in Canada. A number of ships traverse the Atlantic intracoastal waterway: the *Newport Clipper* leaves Annapolis, Maryland, for Savannah, Georgia, at some times during the year and in cooler weather she plies the waters between ports farther south on the coast—Palm Beach and St. Augustine, Florida. The *America* runs from Hilton Head, South Carolina, through Lake Okeechobee, Florida, to Fort Myers, Florida. Other ships follow a similar pattern, traveling to northern ports in warmer weather and southern ports in the winter. Likewise, this is true of the West Coast, where ships such as the *Royal Princess* maintain an itinerary out of San Francisco for Alaska and then return to Vancouver during the warmer months. As with most ships, which must remain active and produce income, in winter the *Royal Princess* sails in southern climates.

A number of inland river cruises exist. The beautiful and historical *Delta Queen* and its modern sister ship the *Mississippi Queen* regularly paddle the Mississippi. The *Glacier Bay Explorer* provides inland water cruising on the West Coast in the Sacramento to San Francisco area. Further north the *Pacific Northwest Explorer* regularly leaves Portland, Oregon, in the spring and fall for a tour of inland waters.

If long periods of time away from home are a concern, there are many cruises that run for only a few days. Some are just three days, such as the *Canadian Princess*, which runs from Kingston to Brockville in Canada. And the Hudson River Day Line has a one-day cruise from New York City to West Point Military Academy and back.

Most large ports have undergone a major renaissance, and almost all offer short cruises—usually for a couple of hours—to tour the port area. For example, the *Spirit of Philadelphia* operates out of Penn's Landing in Philadelphia with a number of daily cruises; the *Spirit of New Jersey*, which calls Weehawken, New Jersey, its home port, sails the Hudson River daily; the Circle Line regularly takes visitors on a water tour around New York City; and

Miami's *Dixie Belle*, a paddle wheeler, has patrolled the inland waters with three cruises daily since 1950! These offer some opportunities for part-time and summer jobs for persons wishing to explore a cruise career afloat. Not only will you get the flavor of shipboard life, but you will also gain insight into some of the careers available. However, there are major differences between ship activities in the harbor and those at sea; a visit to a cruise ship when in port will quickly make these evident. Size is one factor. On a recent visit to the New York harbor, I overheard someone say, "Look at how big that cruise ship is." I said, "Wait until you see the rest." Shortly, other ships appeared, and the visitor remarked that they were indeed huge. The newest cruise ships almost dwarf those built just a few years ago.

A word of caution about cruise ship careers: some ships hire mainly employees from the nation of the ship's registry. For example, the *Song of Norway* (Port of Miami) has primarily a Norwegian crew, but it does employ citizens of the United States and Canada.

Ship Lines

Those seriously interested in cruise ship careers may wish to purchase *Worldwide Cruise and Shipline Guide*, a bimonthly publication. Contact:

Official Airline Guides
2000 Clearwater Drive
Oak Brook, IL 60521
www.oag.com

The following are cruise ship lines you may wish to contact if you have specific inquiries:

American Cruise Ship Lines, Inc.
741 Boston Post Road, Suite 200
Guilford, CT 06437
www.americancruiselines.com

American Hawaii Cruises
550 Kearny Street
San Francisco, CA 94108
www.pacificislandtravel.com/hawaii/cruises/american_hawaii.html

Bahama Cruise Line, Inc.
200 Madison Avenue, Suite 500
New York, NY 10016
or
4600 West Kennedy Boulevard, Suite 201
Tampa, FL 33609
www.bahama-cruise.4daycruise.com

Carnival Cruise Lines, Inc.
5225 Northwest Eighty-Seventh Avenue
Miami, FL 33166
www.carnival.com

Chandris Cruise Lines
Chandris Fantasy Cruises
900 Third Avenue
New York, NY 10022

Clipper Cruise Line
7711 Bonhomme Avenue
St. Louis, MO 63105
www.clippercruise.com

Costa Cruises
One Biscayne Tower, Suite 3190
Miami, FL 33131
www.coastacruises.com

Cunard Line, Ltd.
555 Fifth Avenue
New York, NY 10017
www.cunard.com

Delta Queen Steamboat Company
30 Robin Street Wharf
New Orleans, LA 70130
www.deltaqueen.com

Eastern Cruise Lines
1220 Biscayne Boulevard
P.O. Box 010882
Miami, FL 33101

Epirotiki Lines, Inc.
551 Fifth Avenue, Suite 605
New York, NY 10176
www.epirotiki.gr

Great Pacific Cruise Lines
3600 Fifteenth Avenue West, Suite A201
Seattle, WA 98119

Hellenic Mediterranean Lines Company
One Hallidie Plaza, Suite 405
San Francisco, CA 94102

Holland America Line-Westours, Inc.
300 Elliott Avenue West
Seattle, WA 98119
www.hollandamerica.com

International Cruise Center, Inc.
185 Willis Avenue
Mineola, NY 11501

K Lines–Hellenic Cruises
Olympic Tower, Suite 504
645 Fifth Avenue
New York, NY 10022

Norwegian Caribbean Lines
One Biscayne Tower
Miami, FL 33131
www.smartcruiser.com

Ocean Cruise Lines
1510 Southeast Seventeenth Street
Ft. Lauderdale, FL 33316

Pearl Cruises of Scandinavia
1700 Montgomery Street, Suite 320
San Francisco, CA 94111

Premier Cruise Lines
101 George King Boulevard
P.O. Box 573
Cape Canaveral, FL 32920
www.abcinfo.com/premier.htm

Princess Cruises
2029 Century Park East
Los Angeles, CA 90067
www.princess.com

Rhine Cruise Agency
(Representing German Rhine Line)
170 Hamilton Avenue
White Plains, NY 10601
www.cruiseweb.com

Royal Caribbean Cruise Line
903 South America Way
Miami, FL 33132
www.royalcaribbean.com

Royal Cruise Line, Ltd.
One Maritime Plaza, Suite 600
San Francisco, CA 94111

Royal Viking Line, Inc.
One Embarcadero Center
San Francisco, CA 94111

Salen Lindblad Cruising, Inc.
133 East Fifty-Fifth Street
New York, NY 10022

Sitmar Cruises
10100 Santa Monica Boulevard, Suite 1100
Los Angeles, CA 90067

Society Expeditions
3131 Elliott Avenue, Suite 700
Seattle, WA 98121
www.pacificislandtravel.com/specials/cruises/societyexpeditions.htm

Sun Line Cruises
One Rockefeller Plaza, Suite 315
New York, NY 10020
www.sunlinecruises.com

Sundance Cruises, Inc.
520 Pike Street, Suite 2200
Seattle, WA 98101

Western Cruise Lines
150 West Sixth Street
San Pedro, CA 90731

Windstar Sail Cruises
7415 Northwest Nineteenth Street
Miami, FL 33126
www.windstarcruises.com

World Explorer Cruises
550 Kearny Street
San Francisco, CA 94108
www.wecruise.com

Be alert to changes in cruise lines involving mergers, new organizations, and termination of service. The following organization offers updated information on its members' travel services:

Cruise Lines International Association (CLIA)
500 Fifth Avenue, Suite 1407
New York, NY 10110
www.cruising.org

There are two interesting and clever websites that offer information for prospective cruise ship employees. The Real Truth About Cruise Ship Jobs at www.shipjobs.com provides specifics about the application process and includes interesting links. Cruise Line Jobs at www.cruiselinejobs.com offers detailed advice on a number of related topics.

3

OCEANOGRAPHY AND THE MARINE SCIENCES

PERHAPS THE MOST exotic of all the sciences, oceanography captures the attention of all those who love the world of water. Yet few realize what the career involves and how difficult it is for individuals to enter professions associated with it. Most oceanographers have a doctoral degree; marine technicians, that is, the persons who assist oceanographers, often need to have a master's degree. However, some marine technicians have two-year community college degrees; they likewise enjoy their profession.

Typical Careers

Oceanography involves the utilization of many sciences applied to the study of the oceans. It attempts to explain processes taking place in the ocean through the principles of other disciplines, such as biology, cartography, chemistry, geography, geology, mathematics, medicine, meteorology, physics, zoology, as well as others. Basically, oceanographers are professionals who use the sea as their laboratory for scientific study. Some rarely leave their laboratories; others do fieldwork in waters all over the world. Many serve on the faculties of universities, combining teaching and research. As with all professionals, each has a special interest within her or his chosen field. Although some overlap between specialties does exist, the main divisions are usually as follows.

Atmospheric Oceanographers

These scientists, also called *marine meteorologists*, study the relationship between the ocean and the atmosphere. For example, their work might involve analyzing the behavior of unusual weather such as thunderstorms, hurricanes, and waterspouts. Most recently, they have studied the El Niño phenomenon and its effects.

Biological Oceanographers

This field, probably the best known to the public, deals with the study of plant and animal life in the ocean. The interests of these professionals range from the one-celled phytoplankton to the largest of all life-forms on earth—whales. For example, some seek antibiotics from bacteria or fungi, others study new life-forms found around hydrothermal vents such as giant clams and tubeworms. The improvement of sport and commercial deepwater fishing is also a concern of biological oceanographers.

Chemical Oceanographers

These professionals seek to understand the chemical reactions taking place in the sea. Also known as *marine geochemists*, they may study the food chain using radioactive substances. Often they will analyze the composition of pollution so that they can suggest methods of prevention and removal. A growing concern with cleaning up the world's waters makes this field attractive to many.

Geological Oceanographers

These individuals, also known as *marine geologists*, investigate the ocean's floor and the shoreline, studying sediments, mineral content, and oil location. Recent interest in coastal erosion and in extricating minerals from the sea and oil from beneath the ocean floor makes employment opportunities good in this field. Some marine geologists obtain jobs with oil companies.

Physical Oceanographers

Persons in this field investigate physical properties of the ocean, such as the chemical properties of seawater, currents, tides, waves, and the relationship between the ocean and the atmosphere. Some study exotic topics such as the transmission of light and sound in the sea and the rise of ocean levels.

Oceanographic Engineers

These individuals design and build systems used in marine research and operations. They supervise the construction of underwater devices and floating structures such as oil drilling rigs and study the interaction of the sea with such structures.

Marine Policy and Law Practitioners

This field covers the broad spectrum of ocean resource management issues concerning ocean environmental quality. Coastal zone management, fisheries, and marine archaeology are topics of interest to those working in this field. These topics often fall under legislative jurisdiction; consequently judges/lawyers are frequently involved in determining status and procedures. Ginny Broadhurst, a marine program coordinator in the state of Washington, in an interview in the *Marine Advanced Technology Education Newsletter* (winter 2005), reflects upon her career in this area: "I've always wanted to work with people, politics, and science to do a better job of protecting the marine environment." Broadhurst, who has a bachelor's degree in environmental conservation and a master's degree in marine affairs, further states: "I went from shoreline management issues into the nearshore, and now I'm getting into deeper waters." People like Ginny improve the quality of life for all of us.

As the work of oceanographers varies greatly, so do the working conditions. Those employed in laboratories examine organisms, conduct experiments, and analyze data. Others prefer to work in the field (or, in this case, the water). They utilize research vessels to aid them in their work. These men and women obtain samples from the sea and often must don SCUBA diving suits to collect specimens from the deep. Tidal pools, inlets, bays, and rivers also function as natural laboratories.

College and university instructors conduct experiments both in the laboratory and in the sea. Some oceanographers work in administrative and supervisory capacities. They manage research institutes, laboratories, schools of marine science, and new product development in industry.

Marine Scientists

Closely related to oceanographers are marine biologists, who utilize the systematic procedures of the science of biology to study marine organisms. In the words of Professor Larry Harris of the University of New Hampshire, "Marine biology is biology with salt added."

Requirements

A bachelor's degree is the minimum requirement for most persons wishing to enter the field. Consequently, a strong background in high school science and mathematics is particularly important. Many high schools now include marine sciences courses that not only offer career awareness experiences, but also provide a basis for future studies in oceanography. The University Laboratory High School at the University of Hawaii schedules a yearlong marine science course for its students. It has become a model for many schools. Science teachers can obtain information from the following:

Hawaii Marine Science Studies Project
University Laboratory School
1776 University Avenue
Honolulu, HI 96822

Hawaii Institute for Marine Biology
www.hawaii.edu/himb

Two other schools with wonderful marine science programs are:

Fort Hamilton High School
8301 Shore Road
Brooklyn, NY 11209

Marine Academy of Science and Technology
Building 305
Sandy Hook, NJ 07732
http://www.mast.mcvsd.org

Technicians who work under the guidance of oceanographers and marine scientists normally receive their training at a two-year community college or at a trade or technical school such as Lee-ward Community College (Hawaii), Florida Keys Community College, and the Southern Maine Community College. Technicians assist in a variety of chemical and physical tests on waves, current flow, or water analysis. They maintain supplies and equipment in laboratories both on the shore and on research vessels at sea. A typical program is that in applied marine biology and oceanography at Southern Maine Community College, which is described below:

> The program prepares students for jobs as research assistants or technicians. The curriculum emphasizes laboratory and field procedures commonly used by private, state, and federal agencies involved in marine and environmental quality research and monitoring.

The program, which leads to an associate degree, involves various oceanography experiences, including time aboard the school's ship, the *Aqua Lab III*.

Some four-year undergraduate schools have a complete program in marine sciences. Many offer courses; a few provide for a major in oceanography. Students typically take courses like one offered at Oregon State University. Entitled "The Sea," the course carries the following description:

> The basic principles of oceanography as demonstrated by current active research. Topics covered are: the formation of ocean basins, seawater, the atmosphere, and the origin of life; the interactions of the oceans, atmosphere, and climate; the geology of life of sub-sea volcanoes; waves, tides, and phenomena such as El Niño.

Moody College of Marine Sciences at Texas A & M University in Galveston, Texas, has initiated a new program entitled, Marine

Sciences with a License Option: "The program retains the basic physical core of the marine sciences program but leads as well toward a United States Coast Guard License." A person who completes the curriculum can take the United States Coast Guard Examination as a third mate aboard a ship of any gross tonnage upon the oceans.

Combining course work in two areas helps graduates in obtaining a job. Some colleges permit undergraduates to take courses during the summer at their marine laboratories. Some of these schools are Duke University in North Carolina; the Marine Biological Laboratory at Woods Hole, Massachusetts; the University of Texas; Drake University in cooperation with Southampton College (Long Island, New York); Stanford University in California; and the University of Washington.

The University of Southern California (USC) has a fine facility in its Catalina Marine Science Center. Located on the beautiful Santa Catalina Island, twenty-two miles from Los Angeles, the center engages in a wide variety of activities, including undergraduate and graduate teaching and research. The center sports some of the most innovative and contemporary oceanographic equipment.

It should be noted that some marine biologists strongly recommend that undergraduate college students major in biology with an occasional elective in marine biology, and then major in the marine sciences in graduate school. One of USC's master's programs is unique: the Master of Marine Affairs. The program contains a number of options but largely focuses upon marine policy. It provides sound training in management and basic work in marine sciences combined with three areas of emphasis: marine policy, marine law, and marine economics.

Most oceanographers pursue advanced study beyond their college bachelor's degrees. Scripps Institution of Oceanography of the

University of California at San Diego suggests that undergraduate work include the following:

- Mathematics—through integral and differential calculus
- Physics—with laboratory, one year, using calculus in its exposition
- Chemistry—with laboratory, one year
- An additional year in either physics or chemistry
- Biology and geology—minimum of one semester each
- Foreign language—preparation in at least one language (German, Russian, or a Romance language)

Long recognized for its leadership in the field, the University of Miami offers many graduate programs in the marine sciences. "Study of Sedimentation" is typical of courses for those majoring in marine geology and geophysics, and it carries the following description: "Environmental processes, and agents that form, transport, and deposit sediments, and the interpretation of the resulting rocks." Located in an ideal setting, the school's facilities encompass several laboratories and research vessels.

For more information relative to the oceanography/marine science and maitime fields, some very helpful websites include those listed below:

- International Oceanographic Foundation (at the University of Miami): www.rsmas.miami.edu/iof
- Careers in Marine Biology and Oceanography: www-marine.stanford.edu/HMSweb/careers.html
- Questions About Careers in Oceanography: www.ocean.tamu.edu/careers
- Marine Biological Laboratory: www.mbl.edu

The following office provides career education materials:

Communications Office
Sea Grant
Kingman Farm
University of New Hampshire
Durham, NH 03824-3512
www.seagrant.unh.edu

Another good place to find information is *University Curricula in the Marine Sciences and Related Fields*, which contains all college programs in marine science and lists the courses in each major field. It is available free by writing the following:

United States Department of Commerce
National Technical Information Service
5285 Port Royal Road
Springfield, VA 22161

An excellent source of information about marine science careers and anything related to them for western Canada is the website for the Vancouver Aquarium Marine Science Center. You can find it at www.vanaqua.org/education/aquafacts/marinebiologist.html.

Job Outlook

The number of oceanographers worldwide remains small (five to six thousand); however, many persons are employed in related careers. The profession will undoubtedly grow in the future, particularly with expected expansion in private industry. The increased interest in and concern over the oceans will stimulate state and federal governments to increase employment in this field. Presently a large percentage of marine scientists (approximately 40 percent) work for the government. One such opportunity is with the National Oceanic and Atmospheric Administration (NOAA) of the Department of Commerce. NOAA oceanographers work in several very exciting areas: some survey and chart the ocean floor; others study the marine environment and its effect on the distribution and abundance of commercially available fish. Naturally, activities vary with the geography; oceanographers study the species peculiar to the area—salmon or tuna on the West Coast and lobsters or clams on the East Coast. For more information, contact the National Oceanic and Atmospheric Administration:

NOAA
Department of Commerce
Personnel Division
Operations Branch, AD41
Rockville, MD 20852
www.noaa.gov

Many other federal government agencies employ oceanographers. Write to:

Office of Personnel Management
Washington Area Office
1900 E Street NW
Washington, DC 20415

Another large group of oceanographers/marine scientists/educators is employed in academic and research positions in universities and marine science centers. The remainder work in private industry and consulting. Salaries are good to excellent, with ample opportunity for advancement.

Bill Ward is a marine sciences educator/advisor who works in the School of Marine Sciences at the University of Delaware in Lewes,

Delaware. Ward has a background in marine science, biology, and teaching, and he has the opportunity to engage students and teachers in discovering the marine world. Some days find him with a group of students afloat in the Delaware Bay taking water samples; other times he may be conducting summer workshops for teachers who are developing lesson plans in marine education. Bill assists the university in many capacities, such as helping to coordinate the state of Delaware's "Coast Day" and aiding commercial fisherman with various programs and public relations/communication activities. He has also authored a pamphlet entitled *Marine Service Careers*. To find out more, go to www.ocean.udel.edu/seagrant.

Sea Grant Programs

Many colleges conduct and maintain a wide variety of marine science projects under their Sea Grant affiliation. These colleges receive federal and state funding for programs designed to maximize quality of marine life, including everything from recreational swimming to commercial fishing. The following schools can provide career-related information in your area:

Alaska Sea Grant
University of Alaska
P.O. Box 755040
Fairbanks, AK 99775-5040
www.uaf.edu/seagrant

California Sea Grant
University of California–San Diego
9500 Gilman Drive
La Jolla, CA 92093-0232
www.csgc.ucsd.edu

Connecticut Sea Grant
University of Connecticut
1084 Shennecossett Road
Groton, CT 06340
www.seagrant.uconn.edu

Delaware Sea Grant
University of Delaware
Robinson Hall, Room 111
Newark, DE 19716
www.ocean.udel.edu/seagrant

Florida Sea Grant
University of Florida
Box 110400
Gainesville, FL 32611
www.flseagrant.org

Georgia Sea Grant
University of Georgia
Ecology Building, Room 13
Athens, GA 30602-2206
alpha.marsci.uga.edu/gaseagrant

Hawaii Sea Grant
University of Hawaii
1000 Pope Road, Room 223
Honolulu, HI 96822
www.soest.hawaii.edu/seagrant

Illinois/Indiana Sea Grant
University of Illinois
51 Mumford Hall
1301 West Gregory Drive
Urbana, IL 61801
www.iisgcp.org

Illinois/Indiana Sea Grant
Purdue University
Department of Forestry and Natural Resources
1159 Forestry Building
West Lafayette, IN 47907-1159
www.iisgcp.org

Louisiana Sea Grant
Louisiana State University
128 Wetland Resources
Baton Rouge, LA 70803-7507
www.laseagrant.org

Maine/New Hampshire Sea Grant
University of Maine
5715 Coburn Hall, Room 21
Orono, ME 04469-5715
www.seagrant.umaine.edu

Maine/New Hampshire Sea Grant
University of New Hampshire
Kingman Farm
Durham, NH 03824-3512
www.seagrant.unh.edu

Maryland Sea Grant
University of Maryland
0112 Skinner Hall
College Park, MD 20742
www.mdsg.umd.edu

Michigan Sea Grant
University of Michigan
2200 Bonisteel Boulevard
Ann Arbor, MI 48109-2099
www.miseagrant.umich.edu

Minnesota Sea Grant
University of Minnesota–Duluth
2305 East Fifth Street
Duluth, MN 55812
www.seagrant.umn.edu

Mississippi/Alabama Sea Grant Consortium
P.O. Box 7000
703 East Beach Drive
Ocean Springs, MS 39564
www.masgc.org

MIT Sea Grant
Massachusetts Institute of Technology
Building E38, Room 300
77 Massachusetts Avenue
Cambridge, MA 02139
web.mit.edu/seagrant

New Jersey Sea Grant
New Jersey Marine Science Consortium
Building Number 22
Ft. Hancock, NJ 07732
www.njmsc.org/sea_grant/about_seagrant.htm

New York Sea Grant Institute
State University of New York
115 Nassau Hall
Stony Brook, NY 11794-5001
www.seagrant.sunysb.edu

North Carolina Sea Grant
North Carolina State University
Box 8605
Raleigh, NC 27695-8405
www.ncseagrant.org

Ohio Sea Grant
Ohio State University
1314 Kinnear Road
Columbus, OH 43212
www.sg.ohio-state.edu

Oregon Sea Grant
Oregon State University
Administrative Services, A500 G
Corvallis, OR 97331-2131
www.seagrant.oregonstate.edu

Puerto Rico Sea Grant
University of Puerto Rico
P.O. Box 5000
Mayaguez, PR 00681-5000
www.seagrant.uprm.edu

Rhode Island Sea Grant
University of Rhode Island
Narragansett Bay Campus
Narragansett, RI 02882-1197
www.seagrant.gso.uri.edu

South Carolina Sea Grant Consortium
287 Meeting Street
Charleston, SC 29401
www.scseagrant.org

Southern California Sea Grant
Hancock Institute for Marine Studies
University Park
Los Angeles, CA 90089-0373
www.usc.edu/org/seagrant

Texas Sea Grant
Texas A & M University
1716 Briarcrest Drive, Suite 603
Bryan, TX 77802
texas-sea-grant.tamu.edu

Virginia Sea Grant
Virginia Graduate Marine Science Consortium
Madison House
170 Rugby Road
Charlottesville, VA 22903
www.virginia.edu/virginia-sea-grant

Washington Sea Grant
University of Washington
HG-30
3716 Brooklyn Avenue NE
Seattle, WA 98105-6716
www.wsg.washington.edu

WHOI Sea Grant
Woods Hole Oceanographic Institution
193 Oyster Pond Road
CRL 209
Woods Hole, MA 025431525
www.whoi.edu/seagrant

Wisconsin Sea Grant
University of Wisconsin–Madison
1800 University Avenue
Madison, WI 53705-4094
www.seagrant.wisc.edu

The Marine Advance Technology Education Center offers a variety of different programs and information ranging from supporting remote-operated (undersea) vehicles (ROVs) to programs that assist partnerships between marine industries and education. You may write them at:

MATEC
Monterey Peninsula College
980 Fremont Street
Monterey, CA 93940
www.marinetech.org

If you think oceanography and the marine sciences may be in your future, in addition to the suggestions contained in this chapter, read periodicals on the ocean (see the Recommended Reading section at the back of the book), and, most important, involve yourself in some precareer experiences such as those that are covered in Chapter 10.

4

FISHING

PEOPLE IN THIS career love—absolutely love—their hard, demanding work. Consider Michael Bry. He lives in Ocean View, New Jersey, a couple of miles from the Atlantic Ocean. Upon graduation from Upper Merion High School in Pennsylvania, he moved to the South Jersey shore to pursue his career in commercial fishing. He had begun as a mate on a party boat during high school summers. Mike's first full-time job was as a crew member on an offshore tile and swordfish boat. This included weeklong trips to the Hudson Canyon, some ninety miles offshore. After two years, Mike looked for inshore work. He served as a crew member on a lobster boat and also spent one season fishing for sea bass. For a few years, Mike captained a gill-net boat, fishing for bluefish, shad, and weakfish.

Finally, Mike purchased his own gill-net boat, the *Andrea-M*, a forty-two-foot Virginia-style work boat Mike operates out of Sea Isle City, New Jersey. Trading as the A & M Fish Company, Mike wholesales fish to the Fulton Fish Market in New York City, where brokers distribute it nationwide.

When asked what an average day is like, Mike replied, "long." It begins at 4:00 A.M. with coffee and the weather report. If all is as it should be, the boat is iced up for the catch and starts down the creek in the dark, with the help of radar. By daybreak, Mike and one other crew member reach the fishing grounds about six miles away, with color scope on and gill net ready for searching for fish. Mike reads the color scope, where fish appear on the screen in different shapes and colors. A buoy is thrown and circled by twenty-five-hundred feet of net; then the boat is driven into the center and the fish swim into the net (thus, the name *gill net*). Hydraulics help haul the net back into the boat. The catch is handpicked and put into holding tanks of saltwater and ice to keep it fresh and firm. Occasionally, the catch is cleaned and gutted on the trip home to bring a higher price. At the dock, the fish are packed into cartons with ice and loaded on trucks bound for New York. If all goes as planned, the crew is home in time for dinner.

Often regarded as one of the oldest and most honorable of all professions, commercial fishing in recent years frequently has found itself at the center of controversies. The latter have ranged from wars over fishing territory, to accusations of overfishing, to disputes over management of catches, and to the environmentally destructive use of drift nets ("walls of death"), which entangle large numbers of nontargeted fish. On a more positive note, these problems have focused attention on the importance of commercial fishing to regional and national economies and, thereby, have provided support for the individuals and organizations involved.

This occupation has imprinted its mark on the North American landscape from the enchanting fishing villages of the Canadian maritimes and New England to the shipjacks on the Chesapeake Bay to the large tuna ships docked in the San Diego harbor. The state of Oregon alone licenses more than six thousand people to fish commercially!

Fishing has long been a family business in which the trade and its secrets are handed down from parent to child. Entrance to these jobs on small commercial fishing boats is difficult, but it is sometimes possible to sign on with one, expand your knowledge, and perhaps even purchase your own boat or fleet.

Salaries in the commercial fishing industry are dependent upon the type of fishing you do. Offshore fishing includes draggers, longliners, and scallopers. Deckhands on any one of these boats makes an average of $60,000 a year. They work weeklong trips with little break in between almost twelve months a year. Those on factory ships—ships that both catch and process fish—will stay at sea until they catch their limit (all their ship can hold).

Clammers, gillnetters, and lobsterers make up the inshore fishermen. These people make daylong trips, dawn to dusk, nine months of the year on the East Coast, usually March through December. A crew member on an inshore boat makes approximately $40,000 to $80,000 per year. All commercial fishermen are paid a percentage of their catch. They are paid on a scale, the highest percentage to the owner, the next to the captain, then first mate, and on down. Offshore fishing is rated one of the most dangerous occupations; inshore fishing is considered safer. In fact, a recent television program entitled "The Most Dangerous Profession" featured offshore commercial fishing. The book and subsequent film *Perfect Storm* captured the attention of readers and viewers; it featured a fishing crew that was lost at sea in a storm.

Mike Bry loves fishing for a lot of reasons; it's one occupation where the harder you work the more you can make, and as the owner of the boat, Mike can really push for success. "As an outdoor person, life on the ocean is really being away from the crowd," he said. Mike can't see himself doing anything but fishing. When asked if he would recommend fishing to others, he said, "If you love to fish and you're a hard worker, you can't beat it."

There is currently a strong movement among marine economists to help fishermen become good business managers as well as good fishermen. In the words of D. R. Hetchell, editor of *The National Fisherman*, "Unfortunately not every fisherman has the business training needed to operate independently in this modern world." Marine economists conduct workshops for fishermen, providing them with business knowledge and skills. Those considering a commercial fishing career should take business courses in high school or a community college.

Recently fishing has become more a science than an art. Boats use technical equipment to locate schools of fish. Fishermen know far more than their ancestors did about fish behavior, and catching strategies have improved. Much of this technological innovation is a result of a whole new breed of professionals known as *fisheries scientists*. Though not fishermen, these individuals contribute to the welfare of the industry. There exist a number of occupations in the area, and most fall into the following categories.

Educators

Persons working in this area can be placed into one of two camps: those who serve in universities and teach courses in fisheries science, and those who educate the general public about the sea. The latter are called *marine education specialists*. They work for aquaria, colleges, and marine institutes and frequently prepare publications for the media. Many teach programs about the sea for schoolteachers who wish to integrate such information into their own courses. Marine education specialists work with fishing information, oceanography, and coastal zone management. This occupation's professional organization, the National Marine Educators Association, hosts a website with excellent links at www.marine ed.org. Extension agents are educators who prepare reports, deliver talks, give advice to fishermen, and keep up with problems and trends in the industry.

Administrators

Administrators plan programs, coordinate budgets, and execute policies. They meet frequently with government officials (many fisheries administrators actually work in various government agencies) to discuss regulations and ways of improving business. A major responsibility of many administrators is public relations—working to improve fish sales and profit for the groups they serve.

Researchers

Areas of investigation for marine researchers include physiology, ecology, population dynamics, water quality, pathology, limnology, marine biology, and several other fields. Those specializing in fish must rely on related areas of knowledge. Usually a researcher will deal with species from either freshwater or saltwater, but not from both. Those who work with freshwater species frequently are involved in stocking bodies of water within a state. The researcher tries to maximize the success of the stocking program. Saltwater specialists work with all types of species but usually limit their interest to only a few. Some engage in rather exciting activities, such as the study of shark behavior. Maybe you've read or seen on television the results of some of this work.

Often these scientists research mysteries. For example, one phenomenon that has occurred in Alaska in the Bering Sea has been the sometimes abrupt disappearance of king crabs. This periodic disappearance has created havoc with people's lives, the economy, and the town of Dutch Harbor. This Alaskan town has vacillated between boom, as North America's busiest fishing town, and bust!

In another area of the country, Dr. Nancy Targett, a marine biologist at the University of Delaware, has researched artificial bait for the fishing industry. In a recent issue of the *University of Delaware Sea Grant Reporter*, Targett stated that "Horseshoe crabs are such a good bait because they produce a chemical lure." She hopes to find an artificial horseshoe crab bait that works as well as the real one. As scary as it looks, the horseshoe crab is a valuable part of the marine ecology. Contributions such as Nancy's can preserve the horseshoe crab. A good website for more information about this research is www.oar.noaa.gov/spotlite/archive/spot_delaware.html. See Chapter 3 for more on marine science careers.

Management Positions

Managers work to maintain or develop fish populations for recreational or commercial reasons. Persons working in this capacity pay close attention to fish kills, monitor water pollution, estimate seasonal catches, reclaim new fishing grounds, work with conservation groups, and inform the public about the general state of fishing. One type of manager is the fish culturalist.

Fish Culturalists

Fish culturalists, also known as *aqua culturalists*, manage public or private fish hatcheries, applying knowledge of management and fish culturing techniques. This management specialty requires a working knowledge of the nutritional and environmental needs of various species. General duties may involve the overseeing, trapping, and spawning of fish; incubation of eggs; rearing of fry (young offspring); and the movement of fish to lakes, ponds, streams, or commercial tanks. A specific job might entail taking a species native to one area and introducing it in a new area. This is presently being done with Pacific salmon in Lake Michigan.

People working in the fishery sciences have advanced training. Those who serve as assistants or technicians usually have at least an associate degree; many have a bachelor's degree. A typical two-year program resembles that of Ketchikan Community College in Ketchikan, Alaska. In addition to general courses, the following courses are taken in the fisheries science concentration:

Fish Quality Control
Fishing Equipment Repair
Fishing Techniques
Gillnetting
Ground Line
Hydraulic I and II
Marine Design
Marine Wiring I and II
Navigation and Piloting
Outboard Engine Repair
Pot Fishing
Power Mechanics
Purse Seining
Refrigeration
Trolling

Most of the others working in the profession have advanced degrees; some have doctorates, particularly those in research. In addition, federal government positions require a civil service examination. Approximately 135 colleges offer courses in fisheries biology; of these about forty-five offer a major program leading to a degree. If such a program is consistent with your career goals, your high school courses should reflect college preparatory subjects with a science emphasis.

Typical of four-year college-level courses are the following, which form part of the program at the University of Minnesota.

- **Fishery Management**—Covers the fundamentals of population control; use of fishing regulations; habitat development; water quality control; use of artificial stocks for population maintenance; relationship between sport and commercial fisheries, which also includes economic aspects; fundamentals of hatchery practice; and pond management.
- **Fishery Ecology in Polluted Waters**—Covers factors contributing to the degrading of water quality and its influence on fish production; fishery bioassay; setting of standards and determination of criteria for aquatic organisms; administrative problems of pollution abatement; and the biological effects of various pollutants on fish.

In Newfoundland, Canada, Memorial University houses the Fisheries and Marine Institute. The Fishing Technology Unit of the Institute works to improve the viability of fish harvesting through solving problems in the operation of fishing gear and equipment.

In addition to college and university degree programs, some institutions such as Clatsop Community College in Oregon offer certificate programs that focus on specific training for fishermen.

Aquaculture Positions

This chapter will not be complete without a discussion of the explosively growing field of fish farming, also known as *aquaculture* or *mariculture*. This industry involves growing fish in a systematic fashion in both saltwater and freshwater, indoors and outdoors. Aquaculturists conduct development and training programs for those in the business; they often write research proposals and consult with fish biologists and entrepreneurs to promote the industry. While a young industry, it has proven to be economically feasible and has the potential to provide quality protein. Undoubtedly it will continue to expand. Aquaculturists normally have a master's degree (some have doctorates); their educational background usually combines marine biology and business management. Opportunities and salaries appear to be very good; this truly will be a major career of the twenty-first century.

Job Outlook

The employment outlook in fishing ranges from good to excellent, but it is sporadic. State and government positions will probably expand slowly, but qualified personnel are in short supply. The ranks of sport fishermen are expected to expand greatly; in 2000 an estimated sixty-three million anglers fished for a combined 1.3 billion days! This will obviously put a great strain on government fisheries agents and will require considerable expansion of their activities. Additional growth will occur in private industry, as we look to the sea to satisfy the nutritional requirements of the world's population. Off the East Coast alone, it is estimated there are twenty million tons of annual sustainable yield; about five million tons are presently taken.

The crafts and professions related to fishing offer a wide variety of career opportunities. If you enjoy life in coastal areas or on our inland freshwater systems and have an interest in fish, this career area deserves your serious consideration. One note of caution: fishing careers are often demanding, requiring rigorous work under difficult conditions and in isolated locations. You may want to test your interest by visiting a hatchery or a marine science coastal laboratory, or try some involvement activities through the Boy Scouts or Girls Scouts, or in summer jobs.

Sources of Additional Information

Additional information also will prove helpful, and the following are good places to start.

American Fisheries Society
5410 Grosvenor Lane
Bethesda, MD 20014
www.fisheries.org

American Institute of Fishery Research Biologists
1226 Skyline Drive
Edmonds, WA 98020
www.aifrb.org

American Society of Ichthyologists and Herpetologists
National Museum of Natural History
Washington, DC 20560

Environmental Protection Agency
Fourth and M Streets SW
Washington, DC 20460
www.epa.gov

Fish and Wildlife Service
U.S. Department of the Interior
Washington, DC 20240
www.fws.gov

National Fisheries Institute
1730 Pennsylvania Avenue NW
Washington, DC 20006
www.nfi.org

National Marine Fisheries Service
U.S. Department of Commerce
NOAA
Washington, DC 20235
www.nmfs.noaa.gov

National Wildlife Federation
1412 Sixteenth Street NW
Washington, DC 20236
www.nwf.org

Sport Fishing Institute
608 Thirteenth Street NW, Suite 801
Washington, DC 20005

U.S. Department of Agriculture
Fourteenth Street and Jefferson Drive
Washington, DC 20250
www.usda.gov

Also write to the Department of Fisheries in your state; these will be located in the state capital. If you are interested in finding information about opportunities outside of the United States, write the following:

Fisheries Department
Food and Agricultural Organization of the United Nations
Via Delle Terme Di Caracella
Rome, Italy
www.fao.org/fi/default.asp

Fisheries Research Board of Canada
Department of the Fisheries and Oceans
Ottawa, Ontario
Canada K1A 0H3
www.dfo-mpo.gc.ca

5

COMMERCIAL DIVING

PEOPLE'S INTEREST IN the world of water extends to the world beneath the sea. This exotic frontier of hot vents, unusual fish, and magnificent beauty has attracted people of all ages. Not all activities associated with the deep are exciting—some involve tedious manual labor related to commercial enterprises. In fact, the latter tends to be most common.

During his high school years, Dave Bollinger decided to enter the commercial diving field. The opportunity for "travel, high pay, and adventure" attracted him, an experienced SCUBA diver, to this romantic but dangerous profession. After graduation, he enrolled in the College of Oceaneering in Wilmington, California. The program included rigging, applications of mixed gas diving, and underwater welding, burning, and small tool usage. Since entering the field he has engaged in a variety of jobs, such as pipeline repair, contamination diving, cable laying, and others. The starting salaries are more than $40,000 per year, with extra pay for certain work; often the job involves overtime. Dave's advice to those considering this career: "The working conditions are hard; it's a dangerous job and it doesn't take much to die. It is something you should think about for a long time before getting into it."

The field of underwater diving is divided into four basic areas:

1. Skin diving, in which you hold your breath while diving (In practice in North America, most skin divers use snorkels.)
2. SCUBA (self-contained underwater breathing apparatus), in which you utilize a breathing device mounted on your back
3. Snorkeling, in which you use a breathing tube
4. Surface air supply, in which air is pumped to you through a hose from the surface

Recently, a fifth category could be added—bell and underwater-vehicle diving—in which you work below the surface while inside a submersible. This is discussed later in the chapter.

Although some forms of diving have been practiced for many years, it was not until the early 1960s that SCUBA diving moved from the status of hobby to that of profession.

Specific Jobs

Specific jobs in this industry vary greatly in terms of skills and work situations. The following list is just a sample of these jobs.

Anchor and cable inspection
Barge and pier construction and inspection
Cable laying
Coring of the ocean floor
Demolition

Dive resort activities
Diving systems construction, repair, and maintenance
Dredging
Drilling equipment removal
Emergency medical technician diver
Equipment cleaning and installation
Exploration drilling
Fabrication of special equipment
Flotation devices maintenance
Flow-line installation and maintenance
Gas rack operation
Gravity surveying
Grouting
Guideline replacement
Harbor and deck construction
Hyperbaric chamber operations
Injection equipment installation
Instrument use and maintenance
Life support systems construction, operation, repair, and
  maintenance
Marine environmental control work
Marine patrol (law enforcement)
Medical and emergency care for diving illnesses and
  accidents
Oil drilling and oil production equipment installation,
  repair, and maintenance
Operation of one-atmosphere suits, remote-control
  vehicles, and diving bells
Pipeline installation and maintenance
Platform construction
Police activities

Public safety and marine
Rock drilling and blasting
Salvage
Scientific and academic research:
    Marine archaeology
    Sample collecting
    Seismic surveying
    Specimen collecting
    Surface geological appraisal
    Surface mapping
Search and recovery
Sewage-line installation, inspection, and maintenance
Submersible operations
Supervisor
Tool design and testing
Trenching
Underwater diving instructor
Underwater painting
Underwater photography and videography
Underwater welding and cutting
Waterline installation, inspection, repair, and maintenance
Wellhead repair and maintenance

Many of these jobs require additional skills as well as good diving ability. Bob Smith, director of the National YMCA Center for Underwater Activities, makes the point nicely: "Diving can be exploited to further another career. If you have the ability to weld, take photographs, or understand geology, and you combine it with diving, your career can prove interesting and financially rewarding."

One career with considerable appeal is that of full-time diving instructor. This person may engage in full-time teaching, work in an underwater diving shop, or own or manage a school and conduct courses. In this managerial capacity, you might have the following weekly schedule: teach courses on Monday night at the community college, teach two courses on Tuesday and Thursday at the local high school, and offer private lessons at your school's pool on Saturday morning.

Diving instructors often attend school. For example, those attending the NASDS (National Association of Skin Diving Schools) College receive the following training: diving physiology and psychology; prevention, diagnosis, and treatment of diving hazards; cardiopulmonary resuscitation techniques; certification in senior lifesaving; extensive work in surf rescue techniques and lifesaving adaptations to SCUBA; night diving; and deep diving and surf diving techniques. In addition, there are similar studies in teaching methodology, sales and marketing techniques, as well as general management. Linda Ponder, NASDS administrative assistant, reports, "Presently there are at least one hundred positions for qualified diving instructors open within our member SCUBA schools. They are in such demand that we cannot enroll enough students to fill the needs in our NASDS Diving Instructors College."

In some areas, SCUBA divers work on a contract basis with law enforcement officers. These divers are called upon when a person or a piece of evidence must be retrieved from the water. Large city police departments usually have their own marine units that handle such matters. These officers may do regular police work and then swing into action as divers when the necessity arises. In some areas, such as Florida's Dade County, the Police Underwater Unit averages a call a day. The Florida Marine Patrol, a state group, has actually made some underwater arrests in areas such as illicit drug smuggling and lobster poaching! This career offers the opportunity to mesh an interest in police work with diving.

Chester, Pennsylvania, a Delaware River community not far from Philadelphia, maintains a Tactical Waterborne Team, which acts as a SWAT team for river-related problems; it also carries out other functions. As such, the team practices antiterrorist procedures on a regular basis. The team, made up of police officers with an interest in and skills related to inland waters and ports, focuses upon prevention as well as other activities.

In recent years, an expansion of diving opportunities has resulted from the interest of the petroleum companies in offshore oil. This should continue strongly during the twenty-first century. These jobs involve divers with surface air supply or SCUBA. Surface air supply diving generally involves dives of great depths; in fact, one thousand feet below the surface is not unusual. A lifeline runs from the surface to the diver. SCUBA divers generally work at lesser depths and have the advantage of increased mobility. Some colleges, such as Santa Barbara City College, offer a two-year associate degree in marine diving technology. Students take basic diving courses and technical subjects such as fundamentals of electronics and combination welding. Additional course work in oceanography, marine biology, and related general studies rounds out the program.

Undersea Submersible Diving

An area of diving that has received extensive media coverage recently is underwater salvage and treasure hunting. Television's coverage of the *Titanic* has raised great interest in this profession, and, of course, we can try to recover gold doubloons from Spanish galleys wrecked in the Caribbean. It should be noted, however, that few treasure-hunting projects ever raise the advance capital necessary for such a risky business, and of those that do get off the ground, only a few result in finds important enough to return the backers' investment.

Unromantically enough, in many cases the scrap value of a ship's hull and fittings may exceed any possible treasure value. Salvage divers find steady work more readily than their treasure-hunting counterparts. Nothing is wasted in the maritime field. When a ship is too old for commercial oceangoing use, it is often sold and refitted for inland waterways; twenty years later the same ship may be sold for scrap, even if it's lying beneath one thousand feet of water. Salvage divers with specialized training work at discovering and raising these ships.

Another underwater diving specialty receiving attention relates to research. That is, utilizing underwater submersibles to obtain samples of marine organisms or sometimes just for a recreational tour of the deep. Some individuals believe that the cure for many serious human diseases may be discovered in a marine plant or animal found deep in the ocean. Kim Reisenbichler serves as a senior research technician for Monterey Bay Aquarium Research Institute (MBARI). This organization, established in 1987, develops "state-of-the-art equipment, instrumentation, systems, and methods of scientific research in the deep waters of the ocean."

Kim credits his education for his position in such a valuable and interesting career. "I was introduced to oceanographic methodology while obtaining my A.A. degree at Fullerton College [California]. And I learned about biology, physiology, and some electronics while pursuing my B.A. and M.A. degrees at UC Santa Barbara." He strongly suggests, "For those who are contemplating entering this field, I cannot stress enough the need to gain practical experience." Kim has been a sport diving instructor and scientific diver for more than twenty years. He adds, "Good grades are essential— the thing that can set you apart from the pack is work experience along with good grades."

As one of those fortunate people who enjoys the beauty of nature under the sea while operating a remotely controlled vehicle and occasionally a manned submersible, Kim is the envy of many. He contributes to society through developing new sampling techniques for manned and remote vehicles.

California does not have a monopoly on these activities; research activities take place in most waters of the globe. For example, Rutgers University operates LEO (Long-term Ecosystem Observatory) off the New Jersey coast. As part of this system, it maintains an undersea robot! The latter travels in a preprogrammed area collecting data. Speculation exists that someday one of these vehicles might be utilized to provide data from Europa, one of the moons of Jupiter that appears to have an ocean beneath its icy crust—an incredible possibility.

The twenty-first century will demand a wide variety of specialists, from scientists to technicians, as we look to the oceans to provide a sea of knowledge that will benefit people and society.

Schools

Two examples of schools offering programs for those interested in working with diving vehicles are the College of Oceaneering, and the Underwater Vehicle Training Center of the Professional School of Diving of New York. The former institution offers a course entitled "Bell Diving." This program, which requires prerequisite diving course work and experience, covers "the disciplines of bell systems control; gas management; environmental control; communication; life support systems; decompression techniques; emergency procedures; and lock-out diving."

Located in Houston, Texas, the Underwater Vehicle Training Center offers an ROV (Remotely Operated Vehicle) operator/technician course. The program of 320 hours spaced over eight weeks exposes students to a wide variety of training, including handling systems, vehicle propulsion, navigation and positioning, photography, piloting, and leak detection.

A number of schools offer wreck-diving specialty programs. The YMCA course covers topics such as the following:

Ascending and exits
Charter boat etiquette and safety
Dive-master duties
Emergency procedures for decompression sickness
Gearing up
Introduction to wreck diving
Life-support equipment
Marine life inhabitants in and around wrecks
Motion sickness and diet
Preservation of artifacts
Rescue techniques and first aid
Review of hazards of deep diving
State or federal laws on wreck salvage
Wreck conservation and collection of artifacts
Wreck-hunting techniques

Naturally, such a program requires good health and diving expertise as prerequisites to admission. In addition to classroom lectures, many of the courses involve dives at actual wreck sites.

Al Mikalow, director of the Coastal School of Deep Sea Diving in Oakland, California, reports that the commercial diving industry asks three things of a diver: Does the diver know how to use all kinds of equipment? Can the person handle many different kinds of commercial jobs? Can he or she perform these jobs under the most adverse conditions? At most schools the basic course is similar to that of the Divers Academy of the Eastern Seaboard in Camden, New Jersey. The sixteen-week program of 640 hours covers topics such as the following:

Dive-boat seamanship
Diving equipment
Diving physics and physiology
Medical aspects of diving
SCUBA
Techniques and procedures of deep-sea diving
Underwater cutting and welding
Underwater demolition

The Divers Institute of Technology, located in Seattle, Washington, has a program that encompasses twenty-six weeks and 780 program hours. Its curriculum is more detailed than most and includes a segment on underwater television and video recording. Introductory courses are available in many locations around the nation. For information on advanced career-related programs, the following addresses will be helpful:

Coastal Schools of Deep Sea Diving
320 Twenty-Ninth Avenue
Oakland, CA 94601

Divers Academy of the Eastern Seaboard
2500 Broadway
Camden, NJ 08104
www.diversacademy.com

Divers Institute of Technology
P.O. Box 70312
Seattle, WA 98107
www.diversinstitute.com

Florida Institute of Technology
150 West University Boulevard
Melbourne, FL 32901
www.fit.edu

National Association of SCUBA Diving Schools
P.O. Box 17067
Long Beach, CA 90807

National Association of Underwater Instructors
22809 Barton Road
Colton, CA 92324
www.naui.org

National Council of YMCAs
Diving Programs Department
291 Broadway
New York, NY 10007
www.ymcascuba.org

National Polytechnic College of Engineering and Oceaneering
272 South Fries Avenue
Wilmington, CA 90744
www.natpoly.edu

Underwater Vehicle Training Center
10046 Chickasaw Lane
Houston, TX 77401

Some underwater careers are glamorous; a photographer who records the beauty of the undersea world is the envy of us all. Similarly, skippers of charter boats that take people on day-trips and those involved in undersea habitat research can justly claim to lead interesting lives. Likewise, undersea treasure hunters may strike it rich as they prowl the ocean's depths hoping to locate wrecks of sunken ships. However, not all diving is as romantic as you may imagine. One of the reasons for the high salaries in this field is the hazardous nature of the work. Divers often work in cold, murky waters as well as in beautiful blue seas. Several factors influence the success of a diver's work: depth, visibility, current, temperature, and the state of the surface. Another factor worth considering is that it takes three to four times longer to complete a task underwater than it does on land!

Persons wishing to enter this profession have done so through on-the-job experience, training while in the navy, or formal training programs. However, in recent years, formal training has become the principal vehicle for entrance into the profession. The future outlook of diving looks good, particularly for those with complementary skills in other areas. In fact, a worldwide deficit of trained underwater technicians has been predicted as exploration of the oceans expands. Diving employment is also steady with industrial companies (particularly the oil companies), government agencies, and small businesses.

Commercial diving is one of the most glamorous and exciting of water-related careers, and the world beneath the sea offers awesome opportunities.

6

MARITIME TRANSPORTATION

ANDREA WEBER RINIKER, executive director of the Port of Tacoma, Washington, believes, "These are great jobs, and I feel very lucky to have one. They're also jobs that I'd like to attract more women to. This is an increasingly global economy, and I want to see women comfortable in positions related to global trade and global economics." The Port of Tacoma is the sixth-largest container port in the country and one of the largest in the world, handling more than sixteen million tons of cargo a year, largely from Asia. Although women remain underrepresented in maritime transportation, the situation is changing rapidly.

North America's ports, open 365 days a year and twenty-four hours a day, form a vital component of maritime transportation. Port and harbor facilities provide employment for those engaged in the loading and unloading of commercial ships, in the inspection of cargo (particularly since the attacks on the World Trade Center and the Pentagon), in the underwriting of marine insurance, and in related capacities.

Portside Opportunities

Stevedores (*longshoremen*) working in crews, load and unload ships and move cargo in and out of warehouses. Much of the stevedore's work was previously simple human labor, but now many operate heavy equipment such as lift trucks and cranes.

The expansion of containerization has modified many of the stevedore's cargo operations. Some companies have cranes that can lift twenty- to forty-foot containers weighing up to forty tons and then transport them along a 484-foot frontage area. The speed up and down the track is three hundred feet per minute. Despite this trend toward containerization, there are still many opportunities for longshoremen.

Wages vary with the kind of cargo handled; for example, the moving of distress cargo and explosives carries double the hourly rate of general cargo. Cargo that is thirty-two degrees Fahrenheit or below receives a slightly higher hourly rate than general cargo. *Gang bosses* supervise stevedores; that is, each stevedore is a member of a gang and operates as such.

Car loaders perform work related to the loading and unloading of railroad cars, trucks, barges, and containers.

Marine carpenters build grain feeders; lash and strap cargo using chain, wire, or rope; repair shipping pallets; and perform all wood-related work. They also crate and pack cargo.

Ship cleaners perform cleaning operations in the ship's hold. Specifically, they wash surfaces, paint surfaces by hand and by spray gun, clean oil tanks, take inventory, clean and wash decks, clean and check lifeboats, clean quarters, and sort and check laundry.

Timekeepers govern the timekeeping of work performed on ships, piers, terminals, and barges.

In addition to the *mechanics, locker men, gear men, crane operators, truck drivers, guards, watchmen, ship maintenance personnel,* and others who work on the docks, several clerical occupations exist. *Billing clerks* type invoices that list the items shipped and the dates of shipment. *Manifest clerks* compile and type the list of the ship's cargo or passengers for use at customhouses and terminals. *Pilot station clerks* and *dispatchers* keep records of the ships entering and leaving harbors. *Checkers*, generally assigned at the rate of one per gang, note the receiving and delivery of all freight from vessel to pier or marine terminal. Salaries of dock and harbor workers are very good. For additional information contact the following:

International Longshoreman's Association
17 Battery Place, Room 1530
New York, NY 10004
www.ilaunion.org

Steamship lines offer many opportunities ashore; similar to that of most corporations, the employment ranges from executive staff to office clerk and embraces the following range of activities:

Accounting
Administrative
Insurance
Legal
Marketing
Operations
Personnel
Sales
Traffic

Steamship companies also appoint agents in various cities to represent them and administer their activities. If you wished, you could pick almost any major city and find opportunities there in the steamship business.

One unique program exists at Texas A & M, Galveston campus—the Bachelor of Science in Maritime Administration. Students take a curriculum that includes accounting, finance, law, and management combined with solid foundations in English, history, and liberal arts courses. In addition, course work in port operations, brokerage and chartering, maritime law, international trade and finance, and others round out this unique and exciting program.

Administrative and executive personnel work to bolster the success and efficiency of the port. They plan campaigns to attract ships to the port through personal contacts and brochures. For example, the South Jersey Port Corporation, an agency of the state of New Jersey, has considerably improved the tonnage of the Port of Greater Camden.

Each port has an organization (often called the Port Authority) that works for the benefit of shippers, unions, and the improvement of the economy of the port. These authorities also control the activities of the harbor. Several areas have marine trade associations that function as intermediaries in collective bargaining negotiations between shippers and labor unions.

The following association can provide the addresses of port authorities in your area:

The American Association of Port Authorities
1010 Duke Street
Alexandria, VA 22314
www.aapa.ports.org

Also check the following federal government website, which has links to ports: http://marad.dot.gov/related_links.html.

Many harbor workers learn their craft on-the-job. Applicants for stevedore positions should be in good physical condition and have experience; persons with supervisory ability may become gang bosses. Some harbor workers become machinery operators and receive training from experienced equipment operators. Persons interested in technical or clerical positions should take appropriate course work in high school or community college. Previous work experience in an apprentice role also can be valuable. Many harbor administrators have college backgrounds; others have served as ships' officers or have come up through the ranks.

Employment opportunities will expand in the containerization field and are expected to decline in the traditional areas of cargo handling. However, Jim Traynor of the Philadelphia Marine Trade Association reports, "Pessimists continue to predict that containerization will have a profound effect on the number of available jobs, but all we can say is that it has not really happened in Philadelphia."

Ships and Shipping

Moving commercial cargo by water is one of the oldest forms of trade. Raw materials, manufactured products, and liquids and solids travel by ships, barges, and boats. Each vessel, be it a barge loaded with coal and moving down the Allegheny River, a towboat transporting grain along the Sacramento River, a supertanker moving in the Gulf of Mexico, or a containership loading in Mobile, Alabama, must have a crew. Domestic shipping involves travel over the rivers, bays, lakes, and coastal waterways, while deep-sea ships traverse the sea-lanes of the world.

Unfortunately the maritime shipping industry in the United States is experiencing serious problems. The number of United States flagships declines annually. This has had a serious negative effect upon maritime employment. Some seamen are able to obtain only four months of employment a year. On the Great Lakes only about half of the ships remain actively engaged in commerce. On the inland waterways there exist surplus barges. The expansion of containerships has greatly affected employment. For example, a large modern efficient containership with a crew of twenty-one people can replace four smaller ships each with a crew of forty!

Naturally, shipping is affected by world economics; United States flagships, despite a magnificent record of reliability and safety, have difficulty competing with the ships of other nations. The latter pay their crews considerably less.

The United States fleet no longer occupies a preeminent position in world shipping, but it maintains a position of leadership in maritime technology generally, and safety developments specifically.

Recently the world has seen the launching of such amazing new ships as supertankers and LNGs (liquefied natural gas carriers). The late Paul Hall, former president of the Seafarers International Union, explained the situation: "Our industry is in the midst of a major technological revolution . . . We are faced with the problem of crewing radically different ships like the LNG carriers—ships that require new and expanded job skills for proper manning."

Employment opportunities for young people without skills are rapidly disappearing; fortunately, several schools exist to train crew and officers for these new ships and for cruise ships.

The United States has been a commercial trading nation with a long and successful tradition. Even now that the ocean-shipping pace has slowed, our ships have an excellent record for reliability, safety, and environmental protection.

Oceangoing Opportunities

Historically, sailors have led rugged and interesting lives. Their careers took them to the ports of the world, and their work frequently tested their courage and strength. Today ordinary sailors still make up the majority of personnel aboard ships, which are the biggest self-sufficient mobile structures ever constructed. Most merchant seamen are assigned to a specific department and job title. This is a result of collective bargaining agreements between the ship's management, owners, and unions. However, in recent years some personnel have received the rating of general vessel assistant, which allows them to do entry work in any of the three departments aboard ship.

The Deck Department

The beginning position in the deck department is that of *ordinary seaman*. This person functions as an apprentice working under the direction of able seamen in all phases of work, including washing, painting, chipping rust and repainting, scrubbing decks, cleaning personnel quarters, and generally keeping the ship clean. The jobs will vary with the type of vessel. For example, on tankers, the ordinary seaman also will be involved in cleaning the ship's tanks. Often they will help others, stand watch, and relieve the able seamen; the latter steer the vessel under supervision.

The mainstays of the deck force on oceangoing vessels are the *able seamen*. For example, the *Queen Elizabeth II* employs thirty-two able seamen. Making up about one-fifth of all sailors, able seamen must have a thorough knowledge of all parts of the ship and be able to use all gear and deck equipment. They are responsible for all of the deck rigging and machinery, cleaning, and painting. On some ships, they serve as quartermasters or helmsmen that steer the ship. They must steer the vessel according to the direct orders of the ship's officers. Officially, they must understand steering commands, elementary construction and parts of the ship, nautical terms, passing, fog and distress signals, running lights (lights carried on ships by international agreement between sunset and sunrise), the compass, and other subjects.

In emergencies these seamen perform many important tasks. During a fire, they close doors and handle fire equipment. In serious difficulties, they assist with the lifeboats—removing covers, swinging the lifeboats free from the ships, and lowering them into the water. They must hold lifeboat-men's certificates and be expert in their use. Able seamen practice emergency procedures to keep their skill levels high. Upon docking they handle lines, assist with the loading and discharging of cargo, and sometimes clean the cargo compartments.

The *boatswain* (or *bosun*) serves as the highest-ranking seaman in the deck department. As foreman of the deck crew, the boatswain assigns work and supervises general maintenance operations. This person meets with the chief officer to plan the day's jobs, which may involve overhauling the lifeboats or cleaning and polishing the metalwork. Some vessels carry a *ship's carpenter*, who works with other deck department personnel in making repairs. The title originates from the days of wooden ships and doesn't accurately describe the carpenter's real duties, which today may involve replacing broken glass in a porthole, repairing a lock, or fixing a broken anchor. On some ships, *deck utility people* (*deck maintenance people* or *deck/machine people*) perform deck maintenance work under supervision of the boatswain.

The Engine Department

American ingenuity contributed to the development of the steamship and, consequently, to the demise of the sailing ship. First wood, then coal, and finally oil served to fuel these new vessels; a short experiment in commercial nuclear propulsion (the NS *Savannah*, named for the first steamship to traverse the Atlantic) proved too expensive. The move away from sails resulted in a new specialty aboard ship—those who tended the area of the ship responsible for propulsion. Today various specialists care for the engines.

Wipers, the lowest ranking in the department, perform general duties. Wipers clean and help repair engine room equipment. *Oilers* lubricate the moving and wearing parts of the engine machinery. They check oil pressure and flow to prevent engine damage and aid in the overhaul and repair of engines. *Firewater tenders* check and regulate the amount of water in the boilers, inspect gauges, and regulate fuel flow to keep steam pressure constant. The *qualified member of the engine department* (QMED) must be able to perform and assist with all unlicensed machinery work, such as the refrigeration and steering systems, and must know how to operate the new automated engine room consoles.

Aboard tank vessels is the *pumpman*, who assists the cargo officer in handling liquid cargo and in related tasks such as maintaining pumps and valves. The *ship's electrician* services the generator and motors. This person, sometimes called the *chief electrician*, may have the assistance of a second electrician. The replacement of defective lights and fuses, along with other routine electrical repairs, falls within the domain of electricians.

The Steward's Department

Messmates and *utility mates* form the lowest rating within this department. The former set the tables, serve meals, and clean the mess rooms. The latter prepare vegetables and clean cooking utensils and galley (kitchen) equipment. The *assistant cook*, working under the direction of the *chief cook*, prepares the food for cooking. Similarly, the *cook* and *baker*, under the leadership of the chief cook, do all baking and cook all vegetables and hot meals. In charge of the galley is the chief cook. The chief cook directs the preparation and serving of all meals; the orderliness and cleanliness of the galley also fall under this person's direction. The supervision of the department is the jurisdiction of the *chief steward*. Ordering supplies, planning menus, and supervising meals are some of his or her duties. The chief steward, in consultation with the ship's master, authorizes overtime, receives stores, and accepts responsibility for the efficiency of the department. As with other ratings aboard ship, on many new ships some jobs are combined. For example, the chief cook and chief steward have been replaced by a combination chief steward/cook on some vessels.

Education and Training

Some high schools have begun to offer courses for those interested in maritime transportation careers. At this point, most of the courses tend to be marine science offerings. One example of a school with an excellent maritime studies program is the Randal Aerospace and Marine Science High School in Washington, DC, which offers courses in basic seamanship. These are taught in conjunction with the harbor police and include boating, navigation, "rules of the road," boat maintenance, and some maritime law. In the marine engineering course, students are introduced to the maintenance of marine engines, specifically the 671 GM Diesel Generator, while learning the use of basic hand tools and principles of preventive maintenance. Upon graduation, many of the students obtain jobs in marine and maritime industries. Dr. Richard Odgorny, program director, reports that graduates enter such careers as marina steward, fireboat firefighter, deckhand, the navy, sailing instructor, lifeguard, crabbing and fishing apprentice, yacht-basin service-station attendant, marine engine mechanic's helper, boatbuilding, and clerical positions in government agencies. Their salaries tend to be significantly higher than those of average high school graduates. The student population is divided almost equally between men and women.

Several colleges now offer courses for prospective sailors, and the list is growing. Typical of these institutions is Leeward Community College in Hawaii, which provides courses such as advanced seamanship, basic seamanship and marine orientation, and practical shipboard operation. To locate colleges with maritime offerings in your area, work with your school guidance counselor, use college guidebooks, and search the Web. Several programs exist in community colleges. The following represents only a geographic sampling of the many programs across the nation.

Delgado Community College
Fire School
13200 Old Gentilly Road
New Orleans, LA 70129
www.dcc.edu

Leeward Community College
96-050 Farrington Highway
Pearl City, Oahu, HI 96782
www.lcc.hawaii.edu

Santa Barbara City College
721 Cliff Drive
Santa Barbara, CA 93109
www.sbcc.edu

Seattle Central Community College
4455 Shilshole Avenue NW
Seattle, WA 98107
seattlecentral.edu

Southern Maine Vocational Technical Institute
Fort Road
South Portland, ME 04106
www.mccs.me.edu

Suffolk County Community College
Eastern Campus
Speonk Riverhead Road
Riverhead, NY 11901
www.sunysuffolk.edu

The importance of professional training to members of the merchant marine is reflected in the comments of Frank Drozak, former president of the Seafarers International Union:

> A near tragedy was avoided this month by the alertness of the SIU-contracted *Seattle*, and the excellent training in safety techniques many of its crew had received. An engine room fire broke out November 7 while the *Seattle* was in the middle of the North Atlantic. The oiler on watch had been through fire-fighting school, so he knew just what to do when he saw a fire starting in the auxiliary generator. The dayworking wiper, who had also been through fire-fighting school, helped him get the blaze under control . . . the ship was eventually saved, although the fire lasted six hours.

Fire is the greatest safety hazard aboard ship, and modern marine technology has resulted in new and different situations in which fires can break out. Mariners have few options in the event of a fire—they cannot simply walk away from the flames to safety. The potential disaster to human life, the cargo, and the multimillion-dollar ship is great. Training for prevention of fire-related tragedies is a must.

The preceding example is just one illustration of the importance of professional training for a maritime career. Few opportunities remain for the unskilled in today's merchant marine; fortunately, several schools and programs exist for this purpose. More important, every person employed aboard an oceangoing or coastal United States vessel of one hundred or more gross tons must obtain a United States merchant mariner's document issued by the coast guard. Application for the certificate must be endorsed by a recognized maritime school or by a letter of commitment from a shipping company. Today few companies make such a commitment. Coast guard or naval experience also meets this requirement.

One of the best-known professional schools in the industry is the Seafarers Harry Lundeberg School of Seamanship (SHLSS). At this tuition-free school, training is provided in entry or beginning job skills, upgrading to licensed or unlicensed ratings, and specialized, advanced courses. The school focuses its program in three key areas:

1. Providing young men and women who have no maritime experience with the basic skills they will need to serve aboard U.S. flagships or tugs and towboats
2. Providing professional advancement for experienced men and women through career upgrading programs
3. Providing the academic education that is an essential complement to the modern technical skills in today's water transport industries

Part of the curriculum involves training aboard ship. The program includes courses such as the following for each trainee.

- **Vessel Familiarization**. This course is designed to acquaint students with basic seamanship skills and shipboard terminology. Students learn marlinspike seamanship and cargo handling applicable to ocean and inland waters. Safety, watch-standing duties, and work routines also are taught. On-the-job training takes place on the school's ships and tugs.

- **Lifeboat/Water Survival.** This course of instruction leading to a lifeboat-man certification consists of classroom work and practical training. Subjects taught include emergency drills, lifeboat launching and recovery, lifeboat construction, basic compass navigation, life-raft construction, life-raft launching and maintenance, and use of all lifeboat and life-raft equipment.

The SHLSS offers numerous courses for seamen to upgrade and improve their skills. In the engine department, course work may be taken to obtain an endorsement as fireman/water tender. In the deck department, there are upgrade courses for "Quartermaster," and "Radar Observer," and a "Deep-Sea Deck, Ship-Handling Simulator." Advanced courses in the steward department include those for cook and baker, chief cook, and chief steward positions. For additional information, contact the school directly:

The Seafarers Harry Lundeberg School of Seamanship
Piney Point, MD 20674
www.seafarers.org

You can also contact the Seafarers International Union, which administers the school at www.seafarers.org.

Another fine training program is the National Maritime Union (NMU) Upgrading and Retraining Plan. The purpose of the program is "to provide experienced deck and engine department seamen with training in the new skills, knowledge, and techniques required on automated ships." The program also provides training in shipboard service and food preparation, as well as efficient management in the steward's department. The basic program is fifteen weeks long, with specialization taking up to twenty-one weeks. The program is designed for NMU members, not for those just beginning a maritime career. Travel expenses, board, and a stipend are provided. For further information write the NMU at:

NMU Upgrading and Retraining Plan
346 West Seventeenth Street
New York, NY 10011

The following schools offer a variety of programs for those interested in a career afloat:

American Maritime Officers
School of Marine Engineering and Navigation
2 West Dixie Highway
Dania, FL 33004
www.amo-union.org

Calhoon MEBA Engineering School
Route 5, Box 509
Easton, MD 21601
www.mebaschool.org

Houston Marine Training Services
1600 Twenty-Ninth Street
Kenner, LA 70062
www.houston.marine.com

International Organization of Masters, Mates, and Pilots
Maritime Institute of Technology and Graduate Studies
5700 Hammonds Ferry Road
Linthicum Heights, MD 21090
www.mitags.org

Maritime Safety Consultant
Tidewater School of Navigation
207 Granby Mall
Lonsdale Building
Norfolk, VA 23510

Marine Safety International
Marine Air Terminal
La Guardia Airport
New York, NY 11371
www.marinesafety.com

MEBA–AMO Great Lakes School
1 Maritime Plaza
Toledo, OH 43604

Radio Officers Union, District 3
NMEBA (AFL-CIO)
Maritime Electronic Training School
Route 5, Box 509
Easton, MD 21601

Sea School
3770 Sixteenth Street N
St. Petersburg, FL 33704
www.seaschool.com

United States Government Maritime Administration
Eastern Region Fire Training Registrar
26 Federal Plaza, 37th Floor
New York, NY 10278

(Each of the regional offices of the maritime administration offers fire-training courses.)

A variety of other programs exist in the maritime field. The Franklin D. Roosevelt Institute of the Seamen's Church Institute of New York offers a Certificate Program in Maritime Transportation. The program involves six courses, including "Modern Ocean Transportation," "Maritime Law," "Container Control," and "Terminal Operations." For information about this and other programs, contact the following:

Seamen's Church Institute of New York
15 State Street
New York, NY 10004
www.seamenschurch.org

Oceangoing Working Conditions

Working conditions vary with the nature of the route traveled and the type of ship. The workweek is considerably different from that on land. At sea, most sailors are required to work seven days a week, generally in two separate four-hour shifts every twenty-four hours. While persons in the engine room must be able to withstand intense heat, deck workers have to contend with rain and cold. Modern ships have clean, comfortable quarters. On older ships, rooms are shared; on newer ships, each crew member has a room. Meals are taken in the mess hall, and the food is usually plentiful and good. American sailors have some of the highest salaries in the world; they also earn ample overtime. Some Americans work on the ships of other nations or on vessels owned by American companies and registered abroad. Fringe benefits such as insurance and vacation time are liberal, and opportunities for advancement also exist. Additionally, seafarers have the chance to travel the world. However, with the trend toward quick turnaround time in port, touring is limited.

If this lifestyle appeals to you, you can obtain additional information by writing to the various maritime schools and associations.

Merchant Marine Officers

Today's ships, costing in the hundreds of millions of dollars, require expert knowledge and skills on the part of the ships' officers. Modern vessels perform some amazing tasks; some barge ships can carry barges weighing five hundred tons each on three decks, and many containerships carry two 140-foot containers at average speeds of more than twenty-five miles per hour.

In command of every oceangoing vessel is a *captain* or *master*. The captain has complete responsibility for the ship's operation and the safety of the crew, passengers, and cargo. While at sea, the captain has complete authority to run the ship within certain guidelines. In port, the captain may serve as the ship-owner's agent in relations with port officials and may act as paymaster. Captains coordinate water and food supplies, piloting, towing, and stevedoring services.

The head of the deck department is the *chief mate* or *chief deck officer*. This person serves as the captain's assistant in assigning duties to the deck crew and in managing personnel. The chief mate, working with the deck crew, plans and supervises the loading and unloading of cargo and assists the captain and pilot in taking the ship in and out of port. To comply with coast guard regulations on the safe and efficient operation of ships, deck officers must be certified for radar, gyrocompass, and radio directional equipment.

The *second mate*, by tradition, serves as the navigation officer. This person maintains navigational equipment, checks instruments, and makes sure that appropriate, up-to-date charts are available.

Some *third mates* generally function as signal officers. They coordinate loading and unloading the cargo, inspecting lifeboats and lifesaving equipment, and determining the ship's position. Most deck officers serve watch.

The *chief engineer* supervises the engine department and its personnel and has responsibility for the safe and efficient operation of the engines and mechanical equipment. At sea this person oversees the operation of the propulsion system and auxiliary equipment and performs other functions such as calculating fuel consumption.

Serving under the chief, the *first assistant engineer* supervises the engine room personnel. Maintaining equipment and machinery falls under this person's direction. The boiler and any related equipment come under the direction of the *second assistant engineer,* who ensures that proper steam pressure and oil and water temperatures are maintained. The *third assistant engineer* supervises the lubrication of the engine room equipment and distillation of saltwater to freshwater. On some ships, the electrical and refrigeration systems fall into the domain of the third assistant engineer as well. Also serving aboard ship is the radio officer, who sends and receives messages from shore and from other ships. Passenger ships and some freighters may employ a *purser.* This person helps passengers, assists with the paperwork necessary for a ship to enter or leave port, and, in some cases, serves as the physician's assistant.

Certain requirements must be met to enter the ranks of officers. In addition to age and health qualifications, the candidate must have three years of work experience aboard ship or be a graduate of an approved training program. Coast guard examinations test the knowledge of the candidates. To advance in rank, officers must pass progressively more difficult examinations. Although no formal education is required, most officers attend school. The surest way to become an officer is to attend one of the fine programs at the maritime academies.

Maritime academies across the country are committed to preserving and fostering our country's maritime traditions. Their impressive programs—theoretical knowledge combined with practical experience aboard ship—can be immensely rewarding and enjoyable. At the same time, maritime programs are not without challenge, as illustrated by the comments of Gregory Snyder, a former midshipman at the United States Merchant Marine Academy:

> The most difficult challenge in coming to Kings Point was adapting to a complete and radical change in lifestyle. I had to be willing to exert my greatest effort in everything I did. I feel that Kings Point has made me more responsible, more confident, and a much harder worker.

In addition to general studies courses, which are comparable to those at regular colleges and universities, the maritime academies require course work in maritime history, marine chemistry and engineering, oceanography, international trade, all forms of electronic navigation, and cargo operations. Most college students attend class for nine months each year, but maritime academy midshipmen have eleven months of school. The longer program reflects the time necessary for students to obtain their practical training aboard ship.

All maritime academies welcome qualified women candidates. In fact, the Texas Maritime Academy and the Maine Maritime Academy have the joint distinction of having graduated the first women in the history of the U.S. merchant marine. Deborah Doane of Maine and Susan Carter of Texas both graduated in 1976.

For further information on programs, prerequisites, and fees, contact the following:

California Maritime Academy
200 Maritime Academy Drive
Vallejo, CA 94591
www.csum.edu

Great Lakes Maritime Academy
Northwestern Michigan College
715 East Front Street
Traverse City, MI 49686
www.nmc.edu/maritime

Maine Maritime Academy
Pleasant Street
Castine, ME 04420
www.mainemaritime.edu

Massachusetts Maritime Academy
101 Academy Drive
Buzzards Bay, MA 02532
www.mma.mass.edu

New York State Maritime College
State University of New York
6 Pennyfield Avenue
Bronx, NY 10465
www.sunymaritime.edu

Texas Maritime Academy
Texas A & M University
200 Seawolf Parkway
Galveston, TX 77553
www.tamug.edu/corps

United States Merchant Marine Academy
300 Steamboat Road
Kings Point, NY 11024
www.usmma.edu

A superb website entitled Maritime Education contains links to the maritime academies: http://ils.unc.edu/maritime/mared.html.

The programs vary at the above institutions. For example, the Great Lakes Maritime Academy offers two three-year associate of applied science programs: one of the programs leads to a coast guard license as a Great Lakes mate; the other program leads to a coast guard license as a third assistant engineer. New York State Maritime College offers the following academic programs: Marine and Power Systems Engineering, Marine Transportation/Business Administration, Marine Environmental Science, and Naval Architecture, Facilities Engineering, and Humanities. Titles of specialty courses include "Nautical Science—Tugs and Towing," "Marine Transportation—Marine Insurance," "Law—Admiralty Law."

In Canada, Dalhousie University, located in the port city of Halifax, Nova Scotia, offers a unique program entitled, Master of Marine Management. It features courses "on all aspects of the uses of the seas," such as "Coastal Zone Management," "Marine Science and Technology," and "Contemporary Issues in Ocean Management and Development." Go to www.marineaffairsprogram.dal.ca to find out more.

The future of the maritime enterprise promises that those aboard ship or in harbor activities will lead exciting lives. Ships' officers and harbor supervisors will be in the forefront of many new developments. Salaries, working conditions, and vacations are very attractive. Job opportunities are normally fair, and during good times (such as expansion from offshore oil drilling), they are excellent.

Little-known opportunities exist for graduates of maritime programs among the Army Corps of Engineers' dredging operations, as pilots and tugboat captains in the Panama Canal Zone, and aboard research vessels belonging to the National Oceanic and Atmospheric Administration and the United States Navy and Coast Guard. Researchers have predicted a moderate increase in positions in most areas. If certain factors occur, there could be a serious shortage of maritime officers in this century. Those with an interest in the maritime industry and a desire to serve in a position of leadership should seriously consider a career as an officer.

Inland Maritime Careers

A recent issue of the *Shipjack*, the newspaper of the Seafarers Harry Lundeberg School of Seamanship, posed the following question: "What is a quarter-mile long and carries as much as a thirty-five-mile convoy of trucks . . . or as much as twelve 100-ton jumbo railroad cars or as much as sixty 25-ton semitrailers?" The answer: "A tow of fifteen barges!" As this country has become more conscious of the need to conserve energy, water transportation continues to be recognized as extremely efficient. It is for this and other reasons that the domestic shipping industry should experience expansion in the years ahead.

Presently, some 15 percent of America's total transportation moves on its inland waters; 4 percent moves on the Great Lakes (Duluth is the nation's number-one port by tonnage); and 5 percent moves along the coastal ocean routes. During the early years of the twenty-first century, river traffic is expected to increase, Great Lakes traffic is expected to increase, and coastal waters traffic will experience significant growth.

If you have any doubt about this, just visit a major port city; the harbor is a virtual beehive of activity—water taxis, ferries, containerships, sightseeing cruises, party boats, luxury cruise ships, major merchant vessels, and so forth.

Most freight on the inland waterways moves by unmanned, non-self-propelled barges having drafts of six to fourteen feet. The minimum depth of a navigable waterway is nine feet; harbors and channels are maintained at forty feet by the Army Corps of Engineers. Part of our inland commerce also takes place on shallow, self-propelled vessels and tankers; that is, either a tug pulls them or a towboat pushes them. Occasionally a tug will push the barges or carry them alongside.

Barges transport both dry and liquid cargo over the more than twenty-five thousand miles of America's inland waterways. Barge sizes range from five hundred to three thousand tons; however, some oceangoing barges have a capacity of more than thirty thousand tons. The cargoes particularly appropriate to this mode of transportation are raw commodities: petroleum products, chemicals, grains, forest products, and iron and steel.

Increasing demand for water transportation has stimulated the improvement of the waterways, equipment, and technology. Consequently, barge service is safe and reliable. Origin-to-destination speed averages six miles per hour, with some tows making fifteen miles per hour. Many towboats and barges are under construction, and skilled workers are needed to work on them. Water transportation is financially the most efficient mode of travel, especially as oil prices increase.

The attraction of this profession can best be summarized in the words of Charlie Piot. A Princeton graduate, Charlie was drawn not by the financial opportunity of the river, but by his personal interest in it.

I came to the river two years ago, just out of college. I wanted to wear a new shirt for a while, to see things from a different angle. The pattern of my life has been all too much the same: my childhood in the suburbs, my high school years in a private school, my college years in an Eastern university. It was all too narrow and too simple—a well-lubricated rail that, once hitched up to, I could quite easily follow for the rest of my earthly life and never see another side.

So I sought out work on the boats. I often wondered what life was like on those sooty barge tows I'd seen creeping past the St. Louis waterfront. What was the work like? And the men who work with their hands and their bodies to make a living—what were they like? And the river—the one we've all vicariously experienced through Twain—what was its mystique?

I petitioned the offices of several barge lines and landed a job as a deckhand on a towboat that runs the lower Mississippi from St. Louis to New Orleans.

Charlie found the work rigorous and life on the river rewarding; he expanded his original plan of working six months to two years.

Skill, ability, experience, endurance, and a feel for the river are the prime requirements necessary for success in towing.

Personnel

In the towing industry, the *deckhand* serves as a jack-of-all-trades. This position varies widely with the nature and the size of the cargo and towboat. On large riverboats, the deckhand ties together the many barges into unit tows and then breaks them apart upon reaching the destination. On harbor tugs, the responsibility for tying the large ships to the tug also falls to this person. Deckhands usually work six hours on, six hours off. Boatmen usually spend a specified number of days on and off their jobs each month: twenty days on, ten days off is one common arrangement. This type of work schedule combined with the rigorous and sometimes dangerous nature of the work constitute a lifestyle that is not for everyone.

One of the most important positions in the industry is that of *tanker man*. The movement of millions of barrels of petroleum and other liquid cargoes each year has made this a critical and rapidly expanding job. The tanker man has the responsibility for cleanly and safely loading and unloading the cargo. Once under way, the tanker man maintains close surveillance of the liquid, checking pumps and engines. Some people in this position also work in harbors, refueling ocean ships from bunker barges. Knowledge of and adherence to environmental protection standards is important in this job. The handling of hazardous cargo also requires coast guard licensing. This regulation, now being studied, will probably become more stringent.

In general, towboats have two operators: the *captain* or *master* and the *pilot* or *mate*, who serves as the captain's assistant. When under way, the operators each stand two six-hour watches per day. The responsibility for the safe navigation of the vessel falls to them. While on watch they steer the vessel, monitor the radio and radar sets, and fill out the log. The master works aboard oceangoing tugs; pilots often work on harbor tugs. Aboard towing vessels operating on longer routes, a captain, first mate, and second mate are required. They stand two four-hour watches per day. Boats working the western rivers and inland waterways of the Gulf of Mexico employ a *steersman*. This person, usually in training to become a mate or pilot, steers the vessel. On some of the larger boats, an engineer maintains the engine room. Deckhands often perform this function on smaller boats. The *towboat cook* has the responsibility of serving and preparing four meals a day and coffee around the clock for the crew. On small boats, deckhands take turns doing the cooking.

Developing Your Skills

The Seafarers Harry Lundeberg School of Seamanship and a number of regional schools offer education and training programs. SHLSS Inland and Near Coastal programs have courses such as "Rules of the Road," "Ship Handling and Seamanship," "Cargo Handling," and others.

Other regional schools also exist, such as:

Louisiana Marine and Petroleum Institute
P.O. Box 10251
Station 1
Houma, LA 70363

You may wish to write for information from the following:

The American Waterways Operators
1600 Wilson Boulevard, Suite 1000
Arlington, VA 22209
www.americanwaterways.com

Continued slow expansion of the industry has created a concern that sufficient personnel will not be available to staff its expanding positions. In fact, *Waterways Journal*, the industry's magazine, has predicted an increase in personnel. Presently more than fifty thousand people work aboard inland boats and barges, and a similar number find employment in shore activities related to inland shipping. The increasing cost and complexity of barges, tugs, and towboats make the acquisition of specific skills particularly important to persons interested in this career area.

The website for Cal Maritime provides numerous excellent links; go to www.csum.edu.

HILLSBORO PUBLIC LIBRARIES
Hillsboro, OR
Member of Washington County
COOPERATIVE LIBRARY SERVICES

On a smaller scale, a number of schools providing boat-related training exist; for some, these are an entrance to this field. For example, the Annapolis Sailing School/Annapolis Powerboat School offers instruction to recreational boaters in Annapolis, Maryland; St. Croix, Virgin Islands; Marathon, Florida; and St. Petersburg, Florida. It is located at 601 Sixth Street, Annapolis, MD 21403.

In a different vein, the American Sailing Training Association, located in Newport, Rhode Island, takes as its mission, "To provide people from all walks of life with the opportunity to experience seafaring aboard a vessel under sail." For programs it certifies and sponsors, contact http://tallships.sailtraining.org.

As vessels vary greatly, so do careers afloat; all contribute to an enjoyable, rewarding lifestyle.

HILLSBORO PUBLIC LIBRARIES
Hillsboro, OR
Member of Washington County
COOPERATIVE LIBRARY SERVICES

7

SHIPBUILDING

SHIPBUILDING, AS WITH other industries in North America, has taken a new direction; for some regions it might be expensive yacht construction, for others it's work for the navy. Typical of this trend is Bolinger Shipyards, which is currently constructing high-speed, highly maneuverable combat ships for the United States Navy. These ships will operate mainly in coastal waters and port areas. This represents the next phase in a wonderful shipbuilding heritage.

The United States and Canada have had a rich and productive tradition in the field that predates nationhood and has enjoyed many notable successes. Very shortly after its independence, the United States ranked as a world leader in shipbuilding. Later, American steamships captured world attention and, along with British developments, sounded the death knell of wind-powered sailing ships. On the inland waterways, paddle-wheel steamboats reflected the charm and tradition of nineteenth-century rural America. Likewise, Canada has a strong shipbuilding tradition; the Versatile Pacific Shipyards in North Vancouver is but one example.

The development of the submarine represents a genuine American success story. Pioneered during the American Revolution, bolstered by Confederate technology during the Civil War, and presently exemplified by nuclear-powered denizens of the deep, the submarine reflects true American ingenuity.

Shipyards were again put to the test during World War II, when more than five thousand vessels were produced for the war effort. More recently, American shipyards have suffered from neglect. Many now emphasize repair as opposed to construction. Typical is Norfolk Shipbuilding and Drydock Corporation (NORSHIPCO), one of North America's leading ship repair complexes located at the port of Hampton Roads in Virginia (www.norshipco.com).

Historically, ship construction has followed these steps:

1. **Preliminary design phase**. Today's craftsworkers rely heavily on computer-aided design throughout the construction process.
2. **Contract award**. This marks the initiation of the shipbuilding process; it means that a particular shipbuilding company has been designated by the purchaser to build the ship.
3. **Ship start**. Approximately seven months from the awarding of the contract, metal is cut. However, prior to this, months have been spent in ship design by naval architects, marine engineers, drafters, and others. Additionally, plans have been made for expansion of the labor force, purchase of equipment, and sequence of construction.
4. **Slab start**. The first metal cutting is fitted together into modules. Simultaneously, piping, ducts, and wiring are started.
5. **Keel laying**. The keel serves as the backbone of the ship, and a ceremony accompanies its laying. This usually takes

place seven months from slab start. The hull construction continues as each section is added to the vessel.

6. **Launch.** The first test of a ship comes at launching, when it is about 80 percent completed. With great ceremony, a bottle of champagne is broken on the ship's prow and the ship slides into the water or is floated in dry dock.

7. **Dry-docking.** Following the launch, the ship moves to its outfitting dock for the installation of its remaining systems and equipment. While there, the hull is inspected for seepage or leaks. Dry-docking consists of placing the vessel in a floating structure that permits access to the underwater portion for inspection, cleaning, and repairs.

8. **Light off.** This step occurs when the boiler, engines, and generators are ready to be run and tested.

9. **Builder's trials.** After the launching and outfitting, the ship undergoes a series of tests at sea. A crew—along with personnel from the shipbuilder's office—conducts this shakedown cruise.

10. **Acceptance trials.** Experts representing the supplier and the purchaser inspect, examine, and test the ship and its systems. The inspectors put together a list of the ship's deficiencies and corrections are made.

11. **Delivery.** Once the purchasing company is satisfied, delivery is made. The purchaser may make certain enhancements.

The total amount of time involved in the shipbuilding process may be less than a year for a small vessel. For the largest supertanker, construction may take two and a half years, or more.

The relationship between the builder and the purchaser continues until the expiration of all items under warranty. Deficiencies related to faulty yard work will be corrected.

Shipbuilding and ship repairing employ many workers:

Boilermakers
Burners
Carpenters
Chippers/caulkers
Cleaners
Clerks
Computer technologists
Coppersmiths
Cost accountants
Crane operators
Drafters
Electricians
Guards
Inspectors
Machinists
Marine engineers
Mold loftsmen
Naval architects
Painters
Pattern makers
Pipe fitters
Production engineers
Purchasing agents
Riggers
Robotic technicians
Safety inspectors
Sandblasters
Sheet metal workers

Shipfitters
Stenographers
Storekeepers
Truckers
Welders

The modern American shipbuilding industry constructs ships with a very high level of sophistication. The majority of the industry's employees fall into the category of professional or highly skilled men and women. The following are examples of some of these maritime professionals.

Naval Architects

Naval architects prepare designs, specifications, and working plans for commercial merchant vessels, naval ships, docks, oil-drilling rigs, and marine facilities often in cooperation with civil engineers. They make cost estimates and supervise the construction of the ship. They advise on problems occurring during building or repair. Schooling for naval architects should emphasize the sciences, mathematics, computer technology, and mechanical drawing. Good communication (both written and oral) and interpersonal skills are essential to this work because of the diversity of planning and teamwork that is required. Emphasis of college courses should be in marine engineering or naval architecture, possibly with graduate work in similar disciplines or in business. Consult your school counselor, the Web, and college guides for a list of schools that offer course work in this area.

If you wish to major in naval architecture, the following schools offer specific course work:

Department of Naval Architecture and Marine Engineering
University of New Orleans
2000 Lakeshore Drive
New Orleans, LA 70148
www.na-me.uno.edu

Department of Ocean Engineering
Florida Institute of Technology
150 West University Boulevard
Melbourne, FL 32901
www.fit.edu/acadres/dems

Massachusetts Institute of Technology
77 Massachusetts Avenue
Cambridge, MA 02139
web.mit.edu

State University of New York
Maritime College
6 Pennyfield Avenue
Fort Schuyler
Bronx, NY 11542
www.sunymaritime.edu

United States Coast Guard Academy
31 Mohegan Avenue
New London, CT 06320
www.cga.edu

United States Naval Academy
121 Blake Road
Annapolis, MD 21402
www.nadn.navy.mil

University of California
University Avenue and Oxford Street
Berkeley, CA 94720
www.berkeley.edu

University of Michigan
Ann Arbor, MI 48104
www.umich.edu

Webb Institute of Naval Architecture
298 Crescent Beach Road
Glen Cove, NY 11542
www.webb-institute.edu

One of the world's most unique colleges, Webb Institute offers a Bachelor of Science in Naval Architecture. All undergraduate students attend the college on scholarship, and placement following graduation is 100 percent! The school also offers a degree in marine engineering.

Two naval architecture programs typical of the specialized and sophisticated courses taken by students at Webb Institute are described below:

- **Naval Architecture III—Ship Resistance and Propulsion**. Wake fraction, thrust deduction, and propulsive coefficient are presented, and the screw propeller is considered as a propulsion device.
- **Naval Architecture VII—Ship Design I**. The design of a ship to meet a specific set of owner requirements is undertaken. Principal dimensions, form characteristics, powering, stability, freeboard, and capacity are all considered.

As a naval architect, working conditions, salary, and fringe benefits are extremely attractive. Those interested in pursuing this career should be able to meet deadlines, concentrate for long periods, pay attention to details, lead others, and make decisions.

The employment outlook is generally very good; new developments in ship construction and maintenance continue to open new doors. Private shipbuilders, the federal government (navy), and naval architecture and marine-engineering consulting firms are the main employers.

For additional information, write the following:

American Society of Naval Engineers
1452 Duke Street
Alexandria, VA 22314
www.navalengineers.org

The Society of Naval Architects and Marine Engineers
601 Pavonia Avenue
Jersey City, NJ 07306
www.sname.org

Architectural programs do exist for boats. The yacht and small-craft curriculum at Chapman School of Seamanship in Stuart, Florida (www.chapman.org), has courses such as "Hull Design and Construction," "Propulsion and Auxiliary Systems," "Support Systems," and others.

A minor renaissance has occurred in the area of yacht and boat-building; North America specializes in these areas. Consequently, we see the expansion of companies such as Cape Cod Shipbuilding: go to www.capecodshipbuilding.com. For general information on the boating industry—news, boat shows, and related links—go to www.boating-industry.com.

Marine Engineers

Closely related to the work of naval architects is that of *marine engineers*, and the two professionals often work together as a design team. However, the field of marine engineering is broader. It may include work on ships, oil rigs, and dock construction as well as responsibility for maintaining all the machinery on a ship as a licensed ship's officer. In the latter capacity, a marine engineer starts out as a third-assistant engineer and works up to the highest grade—chief engineer—in seven to ten years. Some shipyard-related tasks of marine engineers involve supervision of ship repairs, evaluation during shakedown cruises, and design of boilers as well as propulsion and ventilating systems.

Salaries and working conditions of marine engineers are generally comparable to those of naval architects, as are the necessary personality and academic abilities. The employment outlook for marine engineers is variable. The colleges listed in this chapter for naval architects also offer major programs in marine engineering, with the exception of the University of California at Berkeley. The state and national maritime academies also offer programs for marine engineers.

The National Marine Engineers Beneficial Association (AFL-CIO), 30 Montgomery Street, Jersey City, New Jersey 07302 (www.d1meba.org), represents approximately ten thousand of its members serving aboard ships. This union and participating companies administer the Calhoon MEBA (Marine Engineering Beneficial Association) Engineering School. In its three-year upgrading program, the school aims to train marine engineers who will maintain and operate all machinery and all systems aboard ship, including sophisticated electronic equipment. Additional information may be obtained from the school at:

The Calhoon MEBA Engineering School
Route 5
Easton, MD 21601
www.mebaschool.org

Skilled Crafts

This section summarizes many of the crafts that compose the skilled workforce in the shipyard.

One of the most important operations in the yard is welding, the technique that joins the metal pieces of the ship together. *Metalworkers* of all kinds heat, cut, bend, and shape their materials into parts that will be welded together. As the ship takes form, carpenters prepare a building basin or building ways for the laying of the keel and the subsequent assembly.

Crane operators use huge cranes to lift preassembled parts into place. Prefabrication takes place in the shops in the yard, thus reducing cost. Pennsylvania Shipbuilding (Chester, Pennsylvania) has a unique floating crane, which has an eight-hundred-ton capacity. It's a virtual twenty-three-story skyhook.

Shipfitters see that each piece is correctly located and securely fastened by riveters, welders, and other workers. Chippers trim edges through air arc process.

A new staff takes over following launch, when the ship moves to the outfitting pier. At this point, the engineers and *machinists* prepare, install, and test propulsion equipment. *Electricians, carpenters, boilermakers, sheet-metal workers, painters, plumbers,* and others construct internal systems and facilities.

If you want to get skilled work in the yard, take high school courses related to your interest (electricity, machinery, mechanical drawing, computer-aided drafting and design, carpentry). Employers prefer men and women who have graduated from high school and have had some work experience. Once employed, the new worker begins as a helper (for example, a plumber's helper aids and learns from a master plumber), then proceeds to a formal apprenticeship program for three or more years. Following the apprenticeship, the employee qualifies as a journeyman (not included in all crafts). The final level is master, meaning a fully skilled worker.

Shipyard employees, as skilled workers, earn a good salary and enjoy good benefits. Some specialists with skills receive premium salary. The employment outlook remains fair, since certain segments of the shipbuilding industry are undergoing a mild renaissance. A variety of unions dominate the industry and operate apprenticeship programs in cooperation with shipbuilding companies. For additional information contact the following firms. (Because of the state of shipbuilding, some yards have merged and others have closed, and this trend will continue.)

Avondale Shipyards, Inc.
P.O. Box 50280
New Orleans, LA 70150
www.fas.org/man/company/shipyard/avondale.htm

Bath Iron Works Corp.
700 Washington Street
Bath, ME 04530
www.gdbiw.com

Bollinger Shipyards, Inc.
8365 Highway 308 South
Lockport, LA 70374
www.bollingershipyards.com

General Dynamics Corporation
Pierre Laclede Center
St. Louis, MO 63105
www.gd.com

National Steel and Shipbuilding Company
P.O. Box 80278
San Diego, CA 02138
www.nassco.com

Newport News Shipbuilding
14101 Washington Avenue
Newport News, VA 23607
www.fas.org/man/company/shipyard/newport_news.htm

Norfolk Shipbuilding and Drydock Company
P.O. Box 2100
Norfolk, VA 23501
www.norshipco.com

Rohn Marine, Inc.
P.O. Box 2300
Chula Vista, CA 92012

Additionally, the United States Navy operates several shipyards that employ civilians, such as the one in Pascagoula, Mississippi.

The U.S. Maritime Administration (MARAD) is charged with the mission "to promote the development and maintenance of an adequate, well-balanced United States merchant marine, sufficient to carry the Nation's domestic waterborne commerce and a substantial portion of its waterborne foreign commerce, and capable of serving as a naval and military auxiliary in time of war or national emergency." MARAD also "seeks to ensure that the United States enjoys adequate shipbuilding and repair service, efficient ports, effective intermodal water and land transportation systems, and reserve shipping capacity in time of national emergency." See its website at http://marad.dot.gov. This powerful site offers links on everything from inland waterways and port security to ship building, fishing, and others. You will find a site with a long list of links covering many careers, schools, and programs at www.hal pc.org/-nugent/school.html. Another site—www.propellerclubhq.com—offers some insight into the Propeller Club, an organization that works to support the merchant marine industry. The address is:

The Propeller Club
Old Lee Highway, Suite 101A
Fairfax, VA 22030

8

MILITARY CAREERS AFLOAT

WHEN PEOPLE THINK of military careers involving the sea, the U.S. Navy and Coast Guard obviously come to mind. Here is some specific information about both.

United States Navy

Armed with awesome technology, the navy of the twenty-first century will be smaller in both vessels and personnel. Faced with new demands in addition to its many traditional responsibilities, the United States Navy continues to offer men and women rewarding opportunities with wonderful possibilities for either a career of military service or just one "hitch."

Enjoying its third century of service and commitment to the American people, the United States Navy began its existence during the American Revolution. The function of the navy during wartime is well-known; however, Americans tend to give little thought to its peacetime activities. The navy has successfully responded to both conditions. It has distinguished itself in military encounters with foreign powers, including the two great challenges of the past century.

Although considerably smaller than it was when six thousand ships were in its service at the end of World War II in 1945, today's navy, numbering approximately 288 ships, remains vigilant. More diverse than its earlier counterparts, its current fleet includes not only mammoth aircraft carriers but also small boats that are capable of speeds of more than one hundred miles per hour.

Navy personnel number about 363,000, of which 54,266 are officers and 305,479 are enlisted people; some others are in college Naval Reserve Officers Training Corps (NROTC) programs and at the U.S. Naval Academy. Peacetime naval duties include a variety of research activities, such as those on shark and dolphin behavior, undersea habitat, weather forecasting, weapons development, interpersonal relationships, ship development, space exploration, water pollution prevention, and laser technology. The navy remains available for evacuation in case of natural disasters and political crises and for deployment around the world to maintain security. For example, during the Katrina hurricane disaster of 2005, the navy was called in to assist with the search and rescue operations in the stricken Gulf Coast areas. During noncombat periods, the navy practices a variety of tactics and exercises its weaponry and personnel.

Given its many roles, the navy is a large and complex organization with tremendously varied career opportunities. Currently, there are more than seventy-five job skills open to interested and capable men and women. Navy career positions may be divided into enlisted personnel and officers.

Enlisted Personnel

When new enlistees enter the navy, they usually receive the position of seaman recruit. Advancement is through the ranks in the following order:

Seaman recruit
Seaman apprentice
Seaman
Petty officer, third class
Petty officer, second class
Petty officer, first class
Chief petty officer
Senior chief petty officer
Master chief petty officer

The navy currently provides eight and a half weeks of recruit training with a full schedule of military and technical subjects. All recruits are trained at Great Lakes Naval Training Center (north of Chicago) on Lake Michigan in Illinois.

Recruits spend six months in the navy prior to advancing to apprenticeship in their chosen specialty—construction, fireman, hospital, and others. After sufficient training, they qualify as petty officer, third class. They then advance into one of the following major career areas:

Clerical and administrative
Communications
Construction
Data processing

Health
Manufacturing
Mechanical and repair
Scientific and technical service
Social science
Transportation

The majority of individuals in clerical and administrative jobs work in offices. More than one out of five perform clerical and administrative jobs; others serve as *bookkeepers* or *accountants*. Good opportunities exist for advancement and salary increases in this field; training in computer literacy provided by the navy remains a must.

Disbursing clerks make transactions and keep records of payments and receipts for the navy's personnel and purchasing operations. This work takes place at both sea and shore installations. Qualifications include a good memory, mathematical ability, and attention to detail. More than two thousand people serve in this position in the navy. Personnel people maintain service records and perform related enlisted personnel administration duties. *Yeomen* perform secretarial and clerical tasks and office administrative duties. They order office supplies, operate photocopying and duplicating equipment, and perform related tasks. If you enjoy working in an office with a group of people, this position might interest you. Presently, more than ten thousand persons serve in this capacity.

The navy has many skill groups closely related to civilian communications occupations. People who have a talent in photography, art, writing, and other communications media will enjoy such positions. Some communications personnel have attended college or post–high school programs. Competition is keen in these fields. Salaries vary by rank but are generally good; this fact, coupled with independence and creativity, makes for high job satisfaction. The field also includes *cryptologic technicians, illustrator-drafters, intelligence specialists, journalists, lithographers, musicians,* and—a major area—*radiomen.*

Navy *journalists* gather news about people, events, and activities and prepare stories for publication. They may edit a ship's newspaper, write a press release for a sailor's hometown newspaper, or record an interview for radio broadcast. Some write speeches, arrange public affairs exhibitions, and brief the media on new developments. Consequently, these men and women must have the ability not only to think creatively but also to work well with others, both inside and outside the navy.

Serving as the navy's photography professionals are *photographer's mates.* They cover news stories, prepare audiovisual presentations, and produce television shows. Although there are more than twenty-five hundred of these positions in the navy, placement is limited to the highly qualified. As with all other careers, the people who are chosen for them attend technical schools to develop their photographic skills.

Construction workers build, repair, and modernize residential, industrial, and office buildings as well as roads, airfields, and harbors. Related to this field is the repair work of hull maintenance technicians. These men and women perform the metalwork and carpentry necessary to keep all surfaces and structures shipshape. More specifically, some jobs involve maintaining firefighting equipment, replacing defective piping and plumbing fixtures, and inspecting lifesaving equipment. Obviously, an interest in tools and machines is important, as well as manual dexterity and the ability to perform detailed work. Only qualified applicants are accepted into this rank. *Construction engineers* are helped by *engineering aides.* The latter conduct surveys, prepare blueprints and sketches, and lay out all kinds of construction. Once the actual construction work begins, they aid in maintaining quality control until the project's completion.

The expansion of computer systems to aid in information utilization has not escaped the navy. Data processing occupations fall into two ratings: *data processing technicians* and *data systems technicians*. The former operate computers, write some programs for processing operations, and perform office management functions. The latter adjust and repair digital computers, video processors, tape units, buffers, key sets, digital display equipment, data link terminal sets, and related equipment. As with other careers requiring technical training, assignment may be shore or ship duty.

Health occupations include not only doctors and dentists, but also technicians and assistants. There are many opportunities for careers in this area. For example, *hospital corpsmen* assist medical professionals in providing health care to service personnel and their families. Specifically, they apply first aid, minister to the sick and injured, take and process X-rays, and perform similar health-related duties. A science background proves very helpful. Similarly, *dental technicians* assist dental officers (D.D.S. or D.M.D.) in treating patients. They arrange appointment schedules, instruct patients in oral hygiene, assist in surgery, and prepare materials for fillings.

Manufacturing occupations employ skilled and semiskilled workers. Skilled labor requires considerable training, while unskilled workers normally learn on the job. The navy employs only a small number of sailors as *molders*. Molders work in foundries and operate and maintain the ovens in which molten metals are formed into parts. Physical strength and manual dexterity are important qualifications, and future prospects are good. Steelworkers utilize special equipment to construct or demolish steel structures. They erect or dismantle bridges, buildings, piers, and similar facilities. In performing these tasks, special equipment such as the oxyacetylene blowtorch is used. Those interested in this job should be able to handle tools, equipment, and machines. Career opportunities seem to be good.

Among the fastest-growing fields, both in the navy and society in general, are mechanical and repair occupations. Workers learn their skills on the job or through formal apprenticeship training. Men and women who inspect, adjust, test, repair, and overhaul aircraft engines are rated as *aviation machinist's mates*. They work on both helicopter and jet engines. Excellent opportunities exist in this career area. Machinist's mates maintain and repair ship propulsion equipment such as propellers, pumps, oil purifiers, and reduction gears. They also maintain elevators, air-conditioning equipment, and steering mechanisms. Those interested in mechanical and repair occupations should have the ability to work with machinery and equipment and the strength to perform physical tasks.

Scientific and technical occupations ratings account for a very large percentage of careers in the navy. Some examples are *aviation antisubmarine warfare technician, missile technician, ocean systems technician,* and *torpedo-man's mate*.

One of the important peacetime contributions of the navy lies in weather forecasting. It is the *aerographer's mate* who monitors temperature, wind speed, humidity, and other factors used to predict the weather. Once the data have been collected, they must be plotted and analyzed, often with the help of computers.

Gunner's mates are responsible for the operation and maintenance of guided missile systems, rocket launchers, gun mounts, small arms, and similar armaments. *Operations specialists* operate radar, navigation, and communication equipment in the combat information center near the ship's bridge. Persons in these positions identify ships and aircraft and determine their distance, speed, and altitude. Scientific and technical occupations are probably among the most glamorous in the navy—the kind frequently shown in recruiting films. Opportunities remain good to excellent.

A wide range of careers falls under the heading of service occupations. Included here are *cooks, barbers, police officers*, and *building custodians*. A *mess management specialist* operates kitchen and dining facilities, ordering foodstuffs, preparing menus, and serving meals. Some supervisory people manage the officers' and enlisted personnel's quarters. The management of barber, tailor, and uniform shops comes under the function of the ship's servicemen, who also administer the recreation clubs, retail and commissary stores, and laundry and dry-cleaning plants. These responsible positions require skills in keeping accurate records and dealing with people.

Workers in social science occupations specialize in aiding people with their problems of daily living. For example, *lawyers* provide assistance in matters such as voter registration, indebtedness, wills, taxes, customs, legal forms, and claims filing. Likewise, men and women *career counselors* interview personnel, administer tests, and make recommendations for assignments. They suggest career opportunities and avenues of advancement. In all people-oriented ratings, facility with language and empathy with people are important assets.

Transportation field occupations encompass a large number of naval ratings. Traffic control at airfields and on aircraft carriers is directed by *flight controllers*. These specialists coordinate the safe movement of aircraft with radar information and voice radio. They must remain alert to visibility, weather, and lighting systems. Good eyesight and speaking voice are critical tools to this occupation.

One of the oldest jobs in the navy is that of the *boatswain's mate*, who keeps the outside surfaces of ships in good condition, maintains machinery and equipment on ships' decks, handles cargo, and operates barges, tugs, and small boats. The boatswain's mate also supervises the deck crew in cleaning and painting the ship, and teaches seamanship. In addition to these functions, part of the watch-standing duties includes the actual steering of the ship—in fact, they drive the ship!

For the enlisted person, the navy offers many benefits, not the least of which is training. However, it behooves the prospective recruit to gain all the education possible prior to enlisting. After service in the navy, whether for one hitch or a career, many opportunities become available in civilian life. Most private companies are anxious to hire persons with naval training and experience.

The Naval Officer

The naval officer serves in a position of leadership in the navy. Consequently, a good background in the liberal arts as well as a professional and technical education are particularly important. Most officers obtain their training through the United States Naval Academy, NROTC programs, or the Officers Candidate School (OCS) or Aviation Officer Candidate Schools (AOCS).

The United States Naval Academy

The United States Naval Academy takes as its mission "to prepare midshipmen morally, mentally, and physically to be professional officers in the naval service." The academy is located in Annapolis, Maryland, a beautiful nautical setting near the Chesapeake Bay. The curriculum consists of a typical college program coupled with professional military and leadership training. The variety of majors has expanded greatly in recent years. Seven designated bachelor of science degrees are offered in aerospace engineering, electrical engineering, mechanical engineering, systems engineering, marine engineering, naval engineering, and ocean engineering. Students at the academy may also elect undesignated bachelor of science degrees with majors in the following fields:

Aeronautical engineering
Astronautical engineering
Chemistry
Computer science
Economics
Economics honors
Electrical engineering
English
English honors
General engineering
General science
History
History honors
Marine engineering
Mathematics
Mathematics honors
Mechanical engineering
Naval architecture
Ocean engineering
Oceanography
Oceanography honors
Physics
Political science

Political science honors
Quantitative economics
Systems engineering

The following course descriptions provide a sample of the technical matter studied by midshipmen and midshipwomen:

- **Principles of Aeronautics and Flight.** An introductory course in the theory and practice of atmospheric flight, propulsion, rocket performance, space flight, satellite systems and uses, and other topics in the field of astronautical engineering. It is designed to prepare the beginning aerospace engineering student for future studies and to develop good engineering practices.
- **Naval Engineering.** An introduction to ship systems, including basic methods of ship procurement, construction, and power plant selection. It covers principles of ship stability and operability as related to preventive and corrective damage control.
- **Ship Structures.** A course in structural theory and practice. Topics include longitudinal and transverse strength of the hull girder, bending moments in a seaway, plate theory, development of ship structural design, submarine pressure hull design, and shipbuilding materials.
- **Seakeeping and Maneuvering.** A course in ship steering, maneuvering, motion, and seakeeping. The basic equations of motion for a maneuvering ship and for ship motions in a seaway are developed, and various methods of solution are discussed. The course also covers the experimental aspects of seakeeping and maneuvering.

- **Fundamentals of Naval Science.** Introduction to the basic concepts of seamanship, ship handling, coastal piloting, and engineering. Includes at-sea labs on 108-foot-long yard patrol craft (YPs).
- **Polar Oceanography.** A descriptive course that covers the history of polar exploration as well as the physical ocean-ography and meteorology of the polar regions, with partic-ular emphasis on the role of sea ice in global warming studies. Current DoD polar programs will be reviewed including the following: Deep Freeze, International Ice Patrol, and navy operations such as ICEX and TEAMWORK.

Following the four years of study, the graduate must serve a five-year commitment as an active-duty officer. Additional information may be obtained by contacting the academy at:

Director of Candidate Guidance
United States Naval Academy
117 Decatur Road
Annapolis, MD 21402-5018
www.nadn.navy.mil

NROTC

Many colleges and universities prepare naval officers through NROTC programs. These midshipmen and midshipwomen lead essentially the same campus life as civilian undergraduates. In addi-tion to their normal studies, they must satisfactorily complete spec-ified naval science courses and participate in scheduled drills and summer training periods. Some students receive scholarships and a stipend; in addition, nonscholarship students receive an allowance in their junior and senior years. Upon satisfactory completion of all requirements, candidates receive commissions and must serve four years as officers. For additional information contact the following schools:

Arizona University
Auburn University (Alabama)
Boston University
The Citadel (South Carolina)
College of the Holy Cross (Massachusetts)
Colorado University
Cornell University (New York)
Duke University (North Carolina)
Florida A & M University
George Washington University (Washington, DC)
Georgia Institute of Technology
Hampton University (Virginia)
Illinois Institute of Technology
Iowa State University of Science and Technology
Jacksonville University (Florida)
Maine Maritime Academy
Marquette University (Wisconsin)
Massachusetts Institute of Technology
Miami University (Ohio)
Morehouse College (Georgia)
Norfolk State University (Virginia)
North Carolina State University
Northwestern University (Illinois)
Norwich University (Vermont)
Ohio State University
Old Dominion University (Virginia)
Oregon State University

Pennsylvania State University
Prairie View A & M University (Texas)
Purdue University (Indiana)
Rensselaer Polytechnic Institute (New York)
Rice University (Texas)
Rochester University (New York)
Savannah State College (Georgia)
Southern University A & M College (Louisiana)
State University of New York Maritime College
Texas A & M
Tulane University (Louisiana)
University of California–Berkeley
University of California–Los Angeles
University of Florida
University of Idaho
University of Illinois
University of Kansas
University of Memphis
University of Michigan
University of Minnesota
University of Mississippi
University of Missouri
University of Nebraska
University of New Mexico
University of North Carolina
University of Notre Dame
University of Oklahoma
University of Pennsylvania
University of San Diego
University of South Carolina
University of Southern California

University of Texas
University of Utah
University of Virginia
University of Washington
University of Wisconsin
Vanderbilt University (Tennessee)
Villanova University (Pennsylvania)
Virginia Military Institute
Virginia Polytechnic Institute and State University

Many of the above colleges have "cross-town" relationships permitting students at other colleges to become part of the program at an NROTC school. For more information, contact any of the above listed institutions of higher education; the website www.nrotc.navy .mil offers significant information, too.

Officers Candidate School

Qualified graduates of regionally accredited colleges receive sixteen weeks of training at Officers Candidate School (OCS). Located in Newport, Rhode Island, and Pensacola, Florida, these schools provide basic naval science and indoctrination; successful graduates are commissioned as ensigns. More information may be obtained by calling (800) USA-NAVY or going to www.navy.com.

Naval officers have interesting and challenging careers, both on shore and at sea. Some engage in high-level security research at the Pentagon; others instruct future officers; and still others command nuclear submarines. Officers advance through the following ranks:

Ensign
Lieutenant (junior grade)

Lieutenant
Lieutenant commander
Commander
Captain
Rear admiral
Vice admiral
Admiral

The organization of personnel aboard ship closely resembles that of a war organization. The basic shipboard departments are navigation, operations, weapons or deck, engineering, and supply. The *commanding officer* has absolute authority and responsibility for the ship, subject to the limitations of law and naval regulations. It is the responsibility of the commanding officer to exert every effort to maintain the ship and its personnel in a state of maximum readiness. During military action, the commanding officer must engage the enemy and fight to the utmost of his or her ability. If the commanding officer is absent or unable to fulfill these duties, the next eligible officer in grade assumes command.

The *executive officer* functions as an aide or assistant to the commanding officer. As second in command, this person contributes to maintaining the ship's routines efficiently. Specifically, the executive officer assigns personnel and maintains their records, supervises loading and berthing plans, and oversees morale, welfare, and discipline. The executive officer has several assistants who help plan and perform the work, including the *ship's secretary*, who is responsible for the administration of the ship's correspondence and personnel records, and the *legal officer*, who functions as an advisor and staff assistant to the commanding and executive officers.

Each of the ship's departments is headed by an officer. For example, the *engineering officer* is charged with the operation, care, and maintenance of the propulsion and auxiliary machinery; damage control; electrical devices; repairs to the hull; and similar jobs. Among the several assistants is the *engineering officer of the watch*, who reports any defects of machinery that may affect the proper operation of the ship. Several other officers serve aboard ship in other functions. More specific information may be obtained through the official website of the U.S. Navy at www.navy.mil.

Two additional organizations can provide quality information on the navy—the U.S. Naval Institute and the Naval Historical Foundation. The Naval Institute publishes numerous books and conducts programs that are relative to its mission, "the advancement of professional, literary, and scientific knowledge in the maritime services, and the advancement of knowledge of sea power." The Naval Institute may be accessed at www.usni.org. The Naval Historical Foundation focuses upon the history of the navy with attention to many of its leaders, battles, and related events. Its website can be found at www.history.navy.mil.

United States Coast Guard

The United States Coast Guard, often called the Navy of Mercy, has had a long and distinguished record. Beginning in the early years of the country as the Revenue Marine, it sought to dissuade the flourishing smuggling trade. Today's coast guard came into existence prior to World War I with the merger of the Revenue Marine, the Life Saving Service, and the Lighthouse Service. These latter two functions, generally believed to be the most colorful and glamorous, still form an important part of the coast guard's work.

In this post–9/11 era, homeland security serves as an important priority. Contemporary lifesaving methods utilize highly skilled personnel and the modern technology of speedboats and helicopters. The coast guard also takes care of more than forty-four thousand buoys and channel markers, detects and monitors icebergs, collects oceanographic data, enforces drug interdiction, fights to control maritime pollution, maintains port safety and security, clears ice-blocked shipping lanes, administers safe pleasure-boating programs, enforces the two-hundred-mile Offshore Fish Conservation Act, and maintains military readiness. During an average day, the United States Coast Guard may:

- Board ninety large vessels for port safety checks
- Process 120 seamen's documents
- Seize 209 pounds of marijuana and 170 pounds of cocaine worth $9.2 million
- Board 120 vessels for reasons of law enforcement
- Investigate seventeen marine accidents
- Inspect sixty-four commercial vessels
- Save fourteen lives
- Assist 328 people in distress
- Save $2,490,000 in property
- Service 150 aids to navigation
- Interdict 176 illegal migrants

The coast guard numbers some thirty-five thousand active-duty men and women, eight thousand reservists, and thirty-five thousand auxiliaries. The general ratings categories are as follows:

- Deck and ordnance group
- Hull and engineering group
- Aviation group
- Administration and scientific group

Enlisted personnel attend boot camp in Cape May, New Jersey; following this experience, they enter training programs for a number of specialties. One of the most responsible positions within the deck and ordnance group is that of *quartermaster.* This person reads the charts, signals, and other measurements that affect the vessel's navigation. The safety of the vessel depends upon the quartermaster's skill. In addition to above-average leadership ability, good vision and hearing and strong communication skills are important.

Sonar technicians use sonar equipment to locate submerged objects, reefs, and submarines. They are also responsible for maintaining this equipment.

Several technical specialties fall into the hull and engineering category. For example, one of the fastest-growing jobs in the coast guard is that of the *electronics technician*, who handles the continuous checking and repair of sophisticated electronic equipment such as radar, sonar, and radio receivers and transmitters. *Machinery technicians* work on internal combustion engines, refrigeration, air-conditioning, propulsion machinery, and other equipment. Naturally, computer technologists occupy a dominant position.

Within the aviation group, one finds all the ratings relative to aircraft and their functions. The *aviation electrician's mate* works with basic wiring, power circuits and motors, and the maze of electrical systems aboard aircraft and shore installations. The maintenance of parachutes, small arms, munitions, search and rescue equipment, and similar items falls to the *aviation survival man.*

The administration and science group includes *yeomen, public affairs specialists, storekeepers,* and *radiomen.* Others in this category are the *port security man,* who maintains and controls the safe transfer of dangerous cargoes, and the *marine science technician,* who observes, collects, analyzes, and disseminates meteorological and oceanographic data.

The coast guard maintains an academy (New London, Connecticut) and officer candidate school (Yorktown, Virginia) similar to those of the navy. Courses include liberal arts, engineering, and maritime specialties, with special emphasis on the history and mission of the coast guard. The beautiful sailing ship, the *Eagle*, is used as a training vessel. Upon graduation, the new coast guard officer may receive one of several assignments, from the poles to the tropics. Some typical assignments are:

Aviation
Boating safety
Civil engineering
Data processing
Drug interdiction
Environmental protection
Intelligence
Legal assistance
Merchant marine safety
Military readiness
Naval engineering
Personnel administration
Port safety
Public affairs
Reserve administration
Search and rescue

For further information on coast guard officer training, write to the following:

Director of Admissions
United States Coast Guard Academy
15 Michigan Avenue
New London, CT 06320-9807
www.cga.edu

For the interested individual, the coast guard can serve as the avenue to an exciting and rewarding career with good financial security. As with the navy, advancement in rank brings commensurate salary increases. (For specific officer ranks, see the earlier section in this chapter on the navy.) Pension plans are attractive and former coast guard men and women have many opportunities in the business world because of their skills and experience.

The coast guard also has a program that high school students can enter during the summer of their junior year. For additional information on this program, consult your local telephone directory for the nearest recruiting office, or contact the following:

U.S. Coast Guard Recruiting Center
4200 Wilson Boulevard, Suite 450
Arlington, VA 22202
(800) 424-8883
(800) GET-USCG (to talk to your local recruiter)
www.uscg.mil/hq/recruit/recruit.htm (provides a collection of links
    to all aspects of coast guard life)

Those interested in opportunities relative to the Canadian Coast Guard should contact:

Canadian Coast Guard College
Department of Fisheries and Oceans
200 Kent Street
Ottawa, Ontario K1A 0E6
Canada (613) 993-0215
www.cgc.gc.ca

In addition, the Canadian Coast Guard College, located in Sydney, Nova Scotia, maintains an excellent website for the college and for related topics at www.cgc.ns.ca.

9

MISCELLANEOUS MARINE SCIENCE AND MARITIME CAREERS

"MY JOB IS great, actually sensational; I love the quiet but busy world I photograph, and I'm happy to share it." This is what Maggie Martorell has to say about what she thinks is one of the world's most exciting careers: Maggie explores inner space, photographs it, and then shares it with the public. The world beneath the waves has fascinated people for centuries, and Maggie, a regular visitor to this frontier, is the envy of many. The readers of the *Miami Herald* view Maggie Martorell's photographs regularly. Her profession requires expertise in both photography and SCUBA diving, and it is typical of many marine and maritime careers that merge two specialties to achieve personal satisfaction as well as professional success. Interested individuals should expand their knowledge of photography. The Photographic Society of America (www.psa .photo.org) can help while you obtain SCUBA certification. The underwater kingdom awaits!

To provide a sense of the breadth and variety of maritime occupations across North America, this chapter describes a variety of marine and maritime jobs. These jobs offer interesting work in addition to adequate remuneration. A worthwhile marine science or maritime career can be had anywhere, at many different levels, perhaps in combination with another interest or career, and under all kinds of conditions—if you have the skill and creativity to find or create it. If you are not interested in four or more years of college, some of the careers described here can also be mastered in a community college or at a trade/technical school.

Marine Technicians

One of the career categories receiving renewed attention in the contemporary job market is that of the marine technician. To quote from a recent report prepared by the staff of Monterey Peninsula College, A National Forum on Critical Issues in Marine Advanced Technology Education:

> Marine technicians are individuals who apply science and engineering skills to the marine environment, including the open ocean, coastal regions, estuaries, rivers, swamps, and lakes. They may work on board ships or other vessels, directly underwater (e.g., diving, in submarines), remotely underwater (e.g., ROW), in a marine laboratory, or in any number of other marine and coastal settings. Their work often demands the ability to function safely and efficiently in the marine environment.

These individuals work in a wide range of jobs including:

Aquaculture technician
Boatbuilding assistant
Commercial deep-sea diving specialist

Hyperbaric technician
Marine engine mechanic
Oceanography technician
Submersible operator

Some of these occupations have received coverage in earlier chapters in this book; one career deserves special attention here—that of *marine engine mechanic*.

While he was still in high school, George Nylund began working at the Tuckerton Marina in New Jersey. He worked for two summers as well as after school and on weekends during the school year. In that time he advanced from taking care of small clean-up jobs around the marina to doing tune-ups on the motorboats. After high school graduation, George decided to forego college and open Tuckerton Marine Service. His small company would perform maintenance and repair tasks. Now just a couple of years old, his company has a bright future. Most investments of this nature take at least three years to show a profit. Over the late spring and the summer George works long hours, as do his two part-time assistants. However, during the off-season, he makes his own hours, except for attending the training programs conducted by the various marine engine organizations.

Owning your own company, particularly one in which you have the opportunity to work close to water with a variety of boats, makes for an enjoyable life. However, such an undertaking requires good business acumen (accounting, taxes, government regulations), interpersonal skills, and leadership ability. The latter involves supervising people working for you in a considerate yet structured manner. Leadership also involves decision-making in terms of purchasing equipment and materials, expanding the company, advertising, and similar endeavors.

Pleasure-boating industry sales expand yearly. Annually, millions of Americans use more than ten million outboards. At present, more than six thousand marinas, boatyards, and yacht clubs serve American boaters. Some eighteen hundred boatbuilding firms exist in the United States. Some employ hundreds in their many plants.

This is a major industry requiring many mechanics to service these boats. For specific addresses of boatbuilding companies, go to www.boating-industry.com. This megasite contains links to products and services, jobs, submitting résumés, boat engine prices, company close-ups, publications (past and current), and more.

The industry has expanded so greatly that several colleges in coastal areas and near large bodies of water have begun to offer programs for marine engine mechanics. Typical of these is Florida Keys Community College, which offers a marine diesel technology program. Diesel power is prominent in marine propulsion. Commercial shrimp and fishing fleets, charter boats, ferryboats, yachts, and tugboats typically utilize diesel power. Students can earn a certificate in marine gasoline engine technology or marine diesel technology. The latter is a one-year, thirty-one-semester-hour program that leads to a certificate in marine diesel technology. The school also offers a two-year program in marine propulsion technology leading to an associate degree.

Graduates of both programs take jobs as charter-boat captains, diesel mechanics, master engineers for commercial fishing vessels, and service managers for marine equipment suppliers.

Another Florida school offering several programs for marine technician is the Chapman School of Seamanship in Stuart. One of the programs relative to this topic is Boat and Engine Maintenance, which requires eighty-four hours of instruction. The curriculum focuses on three short courses: "Boat Maintenance," "Marine Mechanical Systems," and "Vessel Systems."

According to a recent *Sea Technology Buyers Guide*, one of the major problems facing Gulf of Mexico workboat owners is the lack of qualified personnel; so the future for some job specialties looks very good.

Community colleges and private proprietary schools (for profit) have taken the lead in the marine technology area. Most feature a combination of classroom and practical experience. Some of these schools include:

Alexandria Technical College (Minnesota)
Bellingham Technical College (Washington)
Cape Fear Community College (North Carolina)
Chapman School of Seamanship (Florida)
Clatsop Community College (Oregon)
Clover Park Technical College (Washington)
Coastal School of Deep-Sea Diving, Inc. (California)
College of Marin (California)
College of Oceaneering (California)
Diver's Academy of the Eastern Seaboard (New Jersey)
Divers Institute of Technology (Washington)
Florida Keys Community College
Gray's Harbor College (Washington)
Great Lakes Maritime Academy (Michigan)
Gulf Coast Community College (Florida)
Indian River Community College (Florida)
Maine Maritime Academy
Maritime Institute of Technology (Maryland)
North Georgia Technical Institute
Peninsula College (Washington)
Prince William Sound Community College (Arkansas)
Saddleback College (California)

Santa Barbara City College (California)
Seattle Central Community College (Washington)
Shoreline Community College (Washington)
Southern Maine Technical College
State University of New York (Morrisville)
Suffolk County Community College (New York)
University of the District of Columbia
Washington County Technical College (Maine)

Monterey Peninsula College (MPC) in Monterey, California, has spearheaded a program to improve the education and training of personnel in this field through working with institutions and organizations. The Marine Advanced Technology Education (MATE) Center at MPC (founded in 1997) hopes to organize a national network to coordinate the education of marine technicians. Its publication, *MATE Newsletter*, contains excellent information on this field as part of its plan to benefit students and faculty. Contact the college at:

MATE Center
Monterey Peninsula College
980 Fremont Street
Monterey, CA 93940
www.marinetech.org

You may also wish to contact the Marine Mechanics Institute, which offers real-world training through its technician programs:

The Marine Mechanics Institute
9751 Delegates Drive
Orlando, FL 32837
www.uticorp.com

If you like being around the water and have a corresponding interest in working with gas engines, visit a boat basin, yacht club, or marina. After walking around the docks and talking with some people, ask for work. Whether or not you are able to gain experience, you may wish to write to the companies that build pleasure-boat engines. In your letter, be sure to request information about the companies, their products, and potential employment.

Nautical Archaeologists

Not a week passes without a major (or minor) "find" under the seas. It could be the *Titanic* in the North Atlantic, a World War II German submarine such as the *U-166* in the Gulf of Mexico, the USS *Monitor* off the Carolinas, or a minor vessel in the Chesapeake or the Great Lakes that will provide a insight into the era as a primary source of history.

One of the most exotic of the occupations in the world of water involves treasure hunting under the sea. This recent science has come to the attention of Americans because of the interest generated by the discovery of a number of sunken ships and treasures. Origins of this field of study date to 1900, when a party of Greek sponge divers accidentally found an ancient shipwreck and salvaged priceless statues from it. For many years marine archaeology remained a crude science; often wrecks were pirated for their booty with little attention to historical artifacts.

The development of SCUBA equipment, undersea vehicles, and systematic procedures for rescuing artifacts from the sea and reconstructing them on shore has contributed to advancing the academic discipline of nautical archaeology. One author and undersea archaeologist describes an experience:

Before ascending, I took a long look around at what undoubtedly was the ruin of a ship. What ship was she? I wondered. Out of what port? Where was she bound, carrying what cargo, and under whose hand? What adventures had she survived before the final one that brought her to the bottom?

The first step in the challenge involves the awesome problem of locating the ship. Once the assembled team has a general idea where a ship may be found, it proceeds to find the vessel. Many times this becomes a difficult task that results in failure. However, if discovered, following the initial examination, a grid of pipes is laid out in the area of the ship. As each piece of wreckage is brought to the surface, it is labeled to facilitate later reconstruction. This field involves serious and painstaking procedures. History thus salvaged from the sea includes items such as cannons, cutlasses, religious objects, water jugs, eating utensils, and even items like lime juicers and dice. Archaeologists use these artifacts and information about the historical period to reconstruct an idea of the ship, its mission, and the people and sailors aboard. Consequently, marine archaeologists contribute to a greater understanding of the past.

Carmen Marquez-Marin operates her own business, Archeo Marine Research, in San Juan, Puerto Rico. In an interview for *Marine Science Careers*, she told of her love for her occupation. "I like having the opportunity to combine my interest in human behavior and my love of the sea while studying how human beings have interacted with the marine environment at different times in history."

The outlook for marine archaeology appears to be good because of a growing general interest in the field and the continued development of undersea technology. However, few opportunities exist; most undersea archaeologists are employed only part-time. Many work in museums and serve on university faculties. Those interested in entering the profession would be well advised to obtain an advanced degree. Diving specialists, who are hired on a part-time basis, fill some of the support positions.

The following college offers a unique master's degree in maritime history and nautical archaeology through its Program in Maritime Studies.

Admiral Ernest M. Eller House
East Carolina University
East Fifth Street
Greenville, NC 27858-4353
www.ecu.edu/maritime

The following universities offer wonderful programs that award M.A. and Ph.D. degrees:

Nautical Archaeology Program
Department of Anthropology
Texas A & M University
College Station, TX 77843-4352
http://nautarch.tamu.edu

Underwater Archaeology Program
Florida State University
Tallahassee, FL 32306
www.adp.fsu.edu/uwarch.html

These programs have made significant contributions to our knowledge of previous societies and cultures and their activities. Their faculty, students, and alumni continue to investigate the deep as they shape the future of nautical archaeology.

Other organizations you may wish to contact include:

The Institute of Nautical Archaeology
P.O. Drawer HG
College Station, TX 77841-1537
http://ina.tamu.edu

The International Institute for Maritime Archaeology
The Bermuda Maritime Museum
P.O. Box MA 273
Somerset, MA BX Bermuda

Ship Restorers

Somewhat related to the career described above is ship restoration, which often involves wooden ships of an earlier era. For example, in America's Bicentennial Celebration Year (1976), an accident occurred during the voyage of the Tall Ships from Bermuda to New York City in which the *Gazela Primiero* was rammed by another ship. Fortunately, a ship's carpenter was able to repair the damaged ship at Mystic Seaport in Connecticut. The incident helped focus national attention on this career. The carpenter was one of just a few people in this country knowledgeable in the skills used decades ago on sailing ships. Several museums are in the process of restoring vessels to their original condition and need people who possess skills in the craft of sailing ship restoration. So important are these persons that museums jealously guard those in their employ. Naturally, these restoration experts receive attractive salaries.

The field of wooden boatbuilding is more active than most would expect. Wooden minesweepers are being built in Wisconsin and wooden shrimpers and fish boats in Florida and Washington state. Along the eastern seaboard and in the northwest, wooden sail and power pleasure boats are under construction. Larger fiberglass pleasure boats have increasing amounts of wood on deck and in the interior. Numbers of older wooden pleasure boats need repair and restoration. Although not a large industry, it requires skilled craftspeople familiar with traditional and modern techniques of building and repair.

Bath, Maine, a cradle of boat and shipbuilding activity for more than three hundred years, boasts a wonderful program in ship preservation skills. This branch of the Maine Maritime Museum trains apprentices, who spend eighteen to twenty-four months at the site, as well as many educators who spend shorter periods of time onboard. The program ties in nicely with the national trend toward using one's hands and has had an excellent response. The museum's apprentices build wooden vessels as they were built in the last century, utilizing time-tested skills and procedures. For example, oils, pine tar, and turpentine are used as preservatives. Anyone interested in this career should contact the following:

Director of Apprenticeship
Maine Maritime Museum
243 Washington Street
Bath, ME 04530
www.bathmaine.com

For general information on maritime restoration, write to:

National Trust for Historic Preservation
740-48 Jackson Place NW
Washington, DC 20006
www.nationaltrust.org

Tri-Coastal Marine
P.O. Box 1049
Galveston, TX 77555

Training for these careers is available at a number of schools. The Norfolk School of Boatbuilding, founded in 1977, offers courses such as "Introduction to Woodworking Tools and Machinery," "Introduction to Traditional Boatbuilding," "Understanding Small Craft Design," and others. Additional information may be obtained on training from the following:

The Apprentice Shop
Box 539
Rockport, MA 04856

The Arques School of Traditional Boatbuilding
P.O. Box 2010
Sausalito, CA 94966
www.arqueschl.org

The Bear Mountain Boat Shop
P.O. Box 191
Peterborough, Ontario E9J 6S8
Canada
www.bearmountainboats.com

Cape Fear Institute
411 North Front Street
Wilmington, NC 28401

Landing School of Boatbuilding and Design
Box 1490
Kennebunkport, ME 04046
www.by-the-sea.com/thelandingschool

Norfolk School of Boatbuilding
Box 371
Norfolk, VA 23501

Northwest School of Wooden Boatbuilding
42 North Water Street
Port Hadlock, WA 98339
www.nwboatschool.org

Philadelphia Wooden Boat Factory
1107 Wharton Street
Philadelphia, PA 19147
www.woodenboatfactory.org

Wooden Boat School
Box 78
Brooklin, ME 04616
www.thewoodenboatschool.com

Maritime Museum Careers

Maritime museums vary greatly; some feature only one ship, such as the museum ship *Norgoma* at the St. Mary's River Marine Center in Sault Ste. Marie, Ontario, Canada; and the N.J. Naval Museum/Submarine USS *Ling* in Hackensack, New Jersey. Many larger museums also exist that feature several vessels, exhibit areas, and a significant staff. Patriot's Point Naval and Maritime Museum (Mt. Pleasant, South Carolina), Independence Seaport Museum (Philadelphia), and San Francisco Maritime Historical Park constitute examples of excellent large facilities. North America has many examples of maritime museums of excellent quality large, medium, and small (see Appendix). Positions vary accordingly.

A curator serves as the professional caretaker of the museum's collections. In a large museum several curators would be employed to oversee various areas, with a director serving as the administrator. In a small museum the curator usually also serves as the manager. In recent years, many museums have added an education director to their staff.

Museums must carefully display their collection to interest and educate the public. Curators and their staffs plan the exhibits of artifacts: ships' anchors, pieces of eight, tools, weapons, photographs, maps, charts, and similar items. Often an organization or individual will lend items for a specific display.

Ship and artifact restoration is an important craft that is related to museum work. The U.S. Naval Academy Museum collection emphasizes the history of the navy (uniforms, ship models, and flags), and the Patriot's Point Naval and Maritime Museum has as its focal point the USS *Yorktown* and the NS *Savannah*. This museum plans dramatic expansion of its facilities. The *Alexander Henry*, a three-thousand-ton icebreaker, forms the focus of the museum of the Great Lakes at Kingston in Ontario, Canada.

Maritime museum careers begin with a strong interest in the sea. Some employees are history buffs; others are professionally trained people with master's degrees or Ph.D.s in history; a few have had course work in museum studies.

There are some museums, such as the magnificent Mystic Seaport Museum in Connecticut, that offer internships in museum studies. Normally these are master's level programs associated with colleges. The work generally takes place indoors and offers opportunities to work with historical artifacts as well as with the public.

Many museums have youth programs. For example, the Independence Seaport Museum in Philadelphia has a long history of summer and year-round student activities. Mystic offers sleepover opportunities for student groups as does Patriot's Point for Girl and Boy Scouts. They and many others offer summer programs. Activities such as these offer an excellent opportunity to test the waters of this profession.

In the Appendix you will find a list of the locations of museums that can provide employment opportunities as well as field-trip experiences to allow a better understanding of marine and maritime activities. Individual museums should be contacted for brochures describing holdings and procedures. You also may wish to contact the following association:

American Association of Museums
1055 Thomas Jefferson Street NW
Washington, DC 20007
www.aam-us.org

In addition the quarterly journal *Sea History* provides updates on museum functions in each issue. A membership is strongly suggested; contact:

The National Maritime Historical Society
5 John Walsh Boulevard
Peekskill, NY 10566
www.seahistory.org

Pilots

Lexie Palmore's college education in commercial art did not prepare her for her present career as a river pilot. Lexie serves as the pilot aboard the famous Mississippi paddleboat, the *Delta Queen*. A graduate of a training program for pilots, Lexie enjoys life on the river but feels the rigors of her demanding schedule: "You have to feel comfortable traveling all the time. I don't have a family of my own, so that isn't a problem for me."

Pilots take ships safely through ports, harbors, and rivers. By law and by custom, when preparing to enter a port, ships must take aboard a harbor pilot to guide the ship into its docking. At pre-arranged locations, harbor pilots meet and go aboard ships. Pilots also guide vessels out of port. For example, ships coming into the port of Philadelphia will be met by a pilot boat out of Lewes, Delaware, just as the ship passes the breakwater and enters Delaware Bay. The pilot possesses intimate knowledge of the harbor and the channel that the ships follow and keeps abreast of changes to maintain the safety of the ship and the harbor (particularly with regard to supertankers) and to avoid running aground. While pilots do give orders, the captain remains responsible for the ship and, consequently, stays in command.

Pilots serve the inland waterways as well as the major coastal harbors. The duties of a pilot on inland waters involve reporting to the captain, responsibility for two six-hour navigation watches and the safety of crew and tow while on watch, communication (navigational reports) with the captain, prediction of vessel fuel utilization, and log entries while on watch.

Many years of experience aboard ships or towboats are necessary to become a river pilot. As with other maritime personnel, pilots must have a license. License specifics vary with the water route over which the pilot will function.

An organization that trains pilots, as needed, is the Seafarers Harry Lundeberg School of Seamanship. This school requires all applicants to show evidence of three years of service in the deck department on steam or motor vessels; eighteen months of this time will have been as an able seaman or the equivalent. Of these eighteen months, one year will have been in the capacity of quartermaster, wheelman, or an equivalent position that included standard regular watches on the wheel and in the pilothouse as part of routine duties. This service will have been on vessels operating on the waters of the class for which pilotage is sought, and 25 percent of this service will have been obtained during the three years preceding the application for licensing.

All candidates must have made the minimum number of normal trips over the route for which the applicants seek licensing as pilots. This minimum is determined by the OCMI (Officer in Charge, Marine Inspection) of the jurisdiction. All candidates must have made one normal trip over the route within six months immediately preceding the date of application. John Wiegman, assistant director at the Lundeberg School notes, "During some periods there exists a surplus of pilots, hence school training ceases."

Admission to membership in a harbor pilot's organization often is difficult. Entrance to the United New York and New Jersey Sandy Hook Pilots Benevolent Association is normally through a relative; each pilot has the right to nominate one candidate at a time. Captain Cornelius Keating, who entered the system without going through a relative, believes it is important that the job be in your blood. "It can get very dangerous. . . . But if you're looking forward to being a pilot [since childhood] you'll go." Harbor pilots undergo a lengthy apprenticeship, but salaries are excellent.

Some special opportunities do exist in this field. On the Delaware River, a fleet of ships (*Good Ship Lollipop*, *Rainbow Yacht*, and *Showboat*) takes people on a tour of the harbor. These smaller versions of the old Mississippi steamboats have young people as their pilots. As high school students, they worked summers as deckhands before becoming pilots. Susan Ardary, owner of the Rainbow Fleet, explains: "They work their way up, get experience on the ship, then apply for their special license for passenger vessels from the coast guard. Of course, they must pass a rigid test before they earn their license."

A career as a harbor pilot permits the individual to combine an interest in ships with a permanent residence on shore. Write to:

Seafarers Harry Lundeberg School of Seamanship
P.O. Box 75, Route 249
Piney Point, MD 20674
www.seafarers.org

Women Afloat

In today's marine and maritime world, women participate in the full range of careers. They serve in numerous oceanography and marine science positions, both in saltwater and freshwater environments. For many years, their contribution to marine ecology has been legend. For example, at North Carolina State University, Lundie Spence works with schoolteachers and students in her capacity as a marine science educator/advisor as a result of her work. Both the educators and their students are growing in their appreciation of the marine environment.

In the maritime world, several women work aboard ships in various capacities. Debbie Doan, one of the first women to graduate from a maritime academy, works for Lykes Brothers Steamship Company. Another, Susan Janis, serves as an officer aboard the *Exxon Boston*, an oil tanker.

In Florida, Nancy Gilligan, armed with her boat captain's license, takes out fishing parties and charter groups. Additionally, she transports sailboats and yachts for their owners.

Onshore, Laurie Seyller serves as a sheet-metal worker at Lockheed Shipbuilding in Seattle. She is just one of many women in the ship construction business.

Joy Wolf has served in numerous executive positions in the field of marine science education. She is director of education for Sea World in San Diego and has served as president of the National Marine Educators Association. The latter is a professional association of educators committed "to make known the world of water, both fresh and salt."

Numerous women serve as enlisted personnel and in the officer corps for the navy and coast guard. They enter through enlistment, the academies, the Officer Candidate Schools, or the Naval Reserve Officers Training Corps (NROTC) and work in various capacities onshore and aboard ship. In the very demanding but romantic world of the sea, one's sex plays no factor in obtaining employment.

Admiralty Law

Although the world of lawyers suffers from overpopulation, one specialty with excellent promise is that of admiralty law. Following undergraduate school, lawyers must attend law school (three years) and pass the state bar examination prior to entrance into the profession. Admission to law school demands very good undergraduate grades and a good score on the LSAT (Law School Aptitude Test). Those wishing to emphasize admiralty law pursue general legal studies in law school, and in the second and third year they take courses in their special area of interest. Only a few schools offer an admiralty or a marine law concentration. One unique graduate law program, entitled Ocean and Coastal Law, exists at the University of Miami School of Law. This curriculum requires an additional year of study in which students take courses such as the following:

Admiralty
Admiralty seminar
Coastal law
International law
Marine insurance

Marine pollution seminar
Ocean law
Water law

Today's legal-minded society does not escape the marine and maritime community; this career offers interesting, valuable, and profitable employment.

Bait and Fishing Shop Owners and Employees

Those with expertise in recreational fishing may wish to consider employment in or ownership of a bait and fishing equipment store. Obvious prerequisites are knowledge of fishing techniques, fish in season, and familiarity with new trends and equipment. People in these careers usually have had a lifelong interest in fishing. If you wish to own or operate a fishing and bait store, business skills and leadership ability will be necessary.

For surfboard, SCUBA, and maritime arts and crafts shops, a similar situation exists; that is, love for and experience with your product must be meshed with sound business knowledge.

Baitfish Catchers

There are millions of men and women who engage in sport fishing annually. Some of these people obtain their own bait; most do not. Consequently, catching these small fish can prove to be a lucrative and enjoyable pastime. Because of the seasonal nature of the work in many locations, another job will be necessary for the winter months. The following excerpt provides an insight into this career:

> My name is Dirty Louis . . . I trap killies to sell to local marinas
> (Manahawkin, New Jersey, area). The business can be lucrative,

with killies or minnows selling wholesale at good prices per quart and forty or more quarts as a decent morning's load. The only requirements for the job are a fast, flat-bottom boat, fifty to seventy-five traps, and a hell of a memory of all the mainland creeks, bay islands, and Sheepshead Peninsula waterways. The secret to trapping killies is to set up in low water and catch the fish as they come into the creeks, but before they can get into the flooded grass with high tide and get other food. Conical traps are baited with bunker, an oily fish, and, with the lack of other eatables in the low creek, the minnows enter the trapping pot. The traps are left in the creeks for one-half to one and one-half hours, depending on location, then pulled and the trapped minnows are transferred to floating boxes that keep them alive . . .

Trapping generally starts on the warmer mainland streams in June and early July then switches to the bay islands in July and then Sheepshead Peninsula near the inlet in August. The same stream should be trapped only once every week or two; thus, a broad knowledge of streams is required. Each trap pulled is a test of one's ability to judge the tide, determine the correct creek, and estimate where in the creek traps are best placed. As the trap quietly breaks the surface, the sounds of tiny slapping minnows crammed in the wire mesh signal a worthwhile catch.

Bait fishing varies widely with geography, temperature, nature of the fish for which the bait will be used, and other factors. On the Atlantic coast, the commercial bloodworm and sandworm can constitute a valuable enterprise. One thing remains constant—this old craft can provide a happy, healthy, and financially worthwhile vocation or avocation.

Marine Insurance Careers

All ocean-related industries require insurance; ships, offshore platforms, cargoes, yachts, marinas, shipbuilding companies, and similar businesses insure themselves against loss. This is not a recent phenomenon. The Insurance Company of North America (now CIGNA), founded in 1792, issued its first policy to cover an American, who was sailing from Philadelphia to Londonderry (Ireland).

A typical person, usually a college graduate, entering the marine insurance field at CIGNA Insurance would spend the first six months learning general insurance and take correspondence courses on marine insurance. After that, the employee would attend the company's formal Marine and Aviation School, approximately four weeks long. Following school, individuals receive their assignments and begin their careers selling insurance, investigating claims, providing safety programs, planning cargo loss control programs, arranging claims settlements, conducting safety inspections, and performing similar activities.

For more information, contact the nearest office of CIGNA or go to www.cigna.com.

Seafood Processing and Marketing Careers

A surprising number of people work in the seafood processing and marketing industry. Presently, more than 150,000 people process the catches of fishermen, and this number increases yearly. The industry is unique not only because of the perishable nature of the fish, but also because of regional eating preferences and sources of fish.

For example, in North Carolina the methods for marketing seafood have changed little over the last several years. The fishermen sell their catch to local packers; the fish, upon icing and packing, are sold to retail markets as far away as New York. Some processors freeze the fish and sell it as a frozen food. Traditionally,

North Carolina has focused on the sale of whole, fresh finfish and shellfish.

Close study of fishing in the Tar Heel state seems to indicate that new ideas will modify the industry. The development of seafood-related industrial parks at key locations along the coast, if properly implemented, will increase the state's processing capacity. Present plans call for expansion of the market into the Midwest. The region, chosen for its potential and proximity to North Carolina, includes eighteen target cities in Minnesota, Wisconsin, Iowa, Missouri, Illinois, Indiana, Michigan, Ohio, Tennessee, and Kentucky. The promotion will feature croaker, gray trout, king and Spanish mackerel, mullet, and rock shrimp. Clearly this campaign will require successful selling techniques. In each city the promoters visit buyers, offer samples, and provide information. Fish marketing specialists meet with newspaper food editors as well as television and radio program directors, distribute brochures, and generally try to educate the public about the qualities of the new species. Such an undertaking, though costly at first, often pays off in later success.

The dramatic increase in aquaculture (fish farming) has greatly affected processing and distribution. For example, New Jersey has begun an oyster farm project in the Cape May/Delaware Bay area. Billed as "Cape May Salt Oysters," these disease-resistant oysters are marketed not only in the greater New Jersey–Philadelphia area but also in New England.

Consumption of fish in the United States expands annually, and predictions forecast continued growth. New seafood restaurants open, seafood menus grow, and home use is on the rise. Norm Angel, executive secretary of the North Carolina Fisheries Association, explains his feelings: "If I were to go into fish marketing today, I would beg, borrow, and steal all the money I could to buy myself a wholly owned freezer and custom cut the fish for the consumer market. . . . This is where the money is."

Academic Careers

A number of careers exist in colleges, universities, and technical institutes as teaching and research faculty. Individuals in these occupations teach courses ranging from oceanography and maritime history to literature of the sea and trends in aquaculture. Those in these university careers have strong educational backgrounds that normally include master's and doctoral degrees. Those teaching technical courses have significant experience in their fields.

These individuals enjoy the marriage of teaching while still participating in the practical world of water. In addition, they possess intellectual curiosity pursuing new knowledge through research and development.

Those interested in careers related to maritime studies (history/humanities) should contact:

The American Neptune
Publications Department
Peabody Essex Museum
East India Square
Salem, MA 01970-3783
www.pem.org/neptune/default.htm

Munson Institute
Mystic Seaport Museum
P.O. Box 6000
Mystic, CT 06355-0990
www.mysticseaport.org

Naval Historical Foundation and Naval Historical Center
Building 57, Washington Navy Yard
901 M Street SE
Washington, DC 20374-5060
www.history.navy.mil

North American Society for Oceanic History
Department of History
East Carolina University
East Fifth Street
Greenville, NC 27858-4353
www.ecu.edu/nasoh

Additionally, a website entitled "Maritime Education" provides an expansive list of the range of careers and schools in this field. You can access it at http://ils.unc.edu/maritime/mared.html. The links range from an ocean classroom based in Cornwall, New York, on the Hudson River, to the Inland Seas Education Association of the Great Lakes.

A number of other unique but limited careers exist in the marine and maritime world. These run the gamut from smokehouse operator (where fish are smoked) to underwater photographer. Those with an interest should read related publications and maintain contacts to remain abreast of career developments in these exciting fields.

10

GETTING YOUR FEET WET

MANY OF THE careers listed in the book offer personally and professionally rewarding opportunities. However, before even embarking on a career, many people need more information and some hands-on experience.

Precareer Experiences

As you prepare for a career in marine sciences and other maritime-related occupations, additional reading will expand your world of knowledge (see Recommended Reading). Organizations in your field of interest offer excellent information. In addition, involvement activities such as an internship are a must. Some other suggestions follow.

Visits

Aquaria, nature centers, marine sanctuaries, and maritime museums offer wonderful awareness and, in some cases, hands-on opportunities for their patrons. Many of these institutions exist in the United States and throughout North America, so a visit is likely not too far away for anyone. Maritime museums offer excellent possibilities for learning experiences. Likewise, many fine aquaria exist (see Chapter 1). For example, the New England Aquarium, located in Boston, provides excellent programs, including multimedia shows, observation of divers feeding fish, touch-and-see aquatic animals, dolphin and sea lion shows, a Sea Explorer post, and independent study opportunities. Most important, many aquaria have specialized programs and volunteer positions for young people. For example, the Vancouver Aquarium boasts a Youth Volunteer Team that is designed "to build future leaders in conservation and career skills"; consult the Youth Volunteer Lounge link on the aquarium's Web page: www.vanaqua.org/helpus/volunteer.html. Organizations such as Sea World offer similar activities specifically for young people. The San Antonio facility offers a Careers Camp for high school students. A week in length, "this once-in-a-lifetime opportunity permits daily interaction with all aspects of marine life." It also offers an Advanced Career Camp. To participate in such programs, contact the education department of the aquarium or oceanarium that interests you. For additional opportunities, you may wish to check out the website of the National Association of Marine Laboratories (NAML) at www.naml.org. Most aquaria have excellent summer programs.

School Programs

If you are a student, ask your teacher to plan marine and maritime studies field trips and encourage your school to integrate these topics into the curriculum. Look into all available marine and maritime courses and programs. Many examples of the types and content of school courses are detailed in this book. Volunteer to aid in setting up the program. Approach faculty members and ask them to sponsor a marine science, SCUBA diving, or maritime careers club; or help to originate a Naval Junior Reserve Officers Training Corp (NJROTC) program. These experiences can be profitable for educators and students. You can take field trips, invite speakers, have discussions, and organize exhibits at the school and in the community. You may even get to take a virtual field trip on the Web; the Jason Foundation for Education hosts an excellent site at www.jasonproject.org.

Opportunities

Several businesses and schools regularly schedule cruises combining recreation and education for young people. Some of these are the Sea Education Association (SEA); Schooner, Inc.; the University of Hawaii's Blue Water Marine Laboratory; the Summer School at Sea of Texas A & M; the Institute for Shipboard Education (Semester at Sea); and Marine Sciences Under Sails.

These typical programs offer college credit and have objectives similar to SEA's Sea Semester, which is a rigorous academic, scientific, and practical experience leading to a thorough understanding of the sea. The Shipboard Education voyage resembles a luxury cruise in which students take courses and visit United States' and foreign ports while enjoying life aboard ship. The college cruises vary in sophistication. Advanced high school students may participate in some programs.

Schooner, Inc., operating on the Long Island Sound, has conducted many fine experiences for teenagers from the greater New York City area. In a program focused on the environment, one student, John Leeds, from Choate/Rosemary Hall, discovered, "My gosh, the slime is really horrible." A classmate observed, "It's like people telling you all about the starving people in India; you really don't know until you see it."

The precollegiate cruises generally have an objective similar to one of Hawaii's programs: the primary purpose of the Blue Water Marine Laboratory program is to increase the awareness, knowledge, and understanding of Hawaii's marine environment in the intermediate and secondary school population in the state, and to do so by offering unique seagoing experiences in ocean studies. Most of the learning activities involve students spending approximately four hours obtaining samples of water and aquatic species, experiencing life aboard ship, and investigating life along the shoreline.

For interesting experiences, have your school contact any of the following:

American Sail Training Association
240 Thames Street
Newport, RI 02840
www.tallships.sailtraining.org

Blue Water Marine Laboratory
George Hall 230
2560 Campus Road
Honolulu, HI 96822

Dirigo Cruises
39 Waterside Lane
Clinton, CT 06413

Institute for Shipboard Education
Taj Mahal Building, Suite 203
P.O. Box 2488
Laguna Hills, CA 92653
www.semesteratsea.com

Marine Sciences Under Sails
P.O. Box 2994
Hollywood, FL 33023

Ocean Challenge
20 Park Plaza, Suite 424
Boston, MA 02116

Ocean Schools Foundation
25 Woodman Road
Durham, NH 03824

Sea Education Association
P.O. Box 6
Woods Hole, MA 02543
www.sea.edu

Schooner, Inc.
60 South Water Street
New Haven, CT 06519

Summer School at Sea
Texas A & M University
P.O. Box 1675
Galveston, TX 77553

If your college does not offer marine science courses, consider a summer program that does. The University of Hawaii at Manoa offers "World Maritime History" and "Maritime Archaeology Techniques." Southampton College of Long Island University plans an excellent selection of courses including "Underwater Photography," "Marine Ecology," "Traditional Maritime Culture," and others.

Think about becoming a student member of the National Marine Educators Association; its publications contain extensive lists of summer opportunities in the marine sciences.

National Marine Educators Association
P.O. Box 1470
Ocean Springs, MS 39566-1470
www.marine-ed.org

To remain current in the maritime world, the following organizations will help:

National Maritime Historical Society
P.O. Box 68
Peekskill, NY 10566
www.seahistory.org

North American Society for Oceanic History
c/o Department of History
East Carolina University
East Fifth Street
Greenville, NC 27858-4353
www.ecu.edu/nasoh

In addition to scanning the newspapers for commercial advertisements, you can find out more about learning experiences aboard ship by consulting Sea Grant educational advisors at colleges and universities offering this program (see Chapter 3).

A number of organizations offer boating/sailing training programs: The Chapman School of Seamanship in Stuart, Florida, schedules Summer Boating for Youth (ages eleven to seventeen); Boat Camp (ages thirteen to eighteen) in San Diego forms part of the Discover the Ocean, Inc., program; and Kid Ship (ages five to fifteen) is located at the Annapolis Sailing School.

A river or harbor cruise can increase your awareness of career activities, and almost every city has one. Contact the following:

Gray Line Sightseeing Association
7 West Fifty-First Street
New York, NY 10019
www.grayline.com

Jean-Michel Cousteau offers a "family camp" on Catalina Island, off the coast of California near Los Angeles/Long Beach. Cousteau, who is the director of the Oceans Future Society, can be contacted via www.oceanfutures.org.

Those interested in maritime transportation will want to look at the Web page entitled Just for Kids and Teens at www.marad.dot .gov/education/kids. It contains a number of fascinating links.

Sea Cadets

The Navy League of the United States, a private organization of individuals interested in the navy, sponsors two youth programs. The activities are aimed at educating and training young people in citizenship and maritime matters, exposing them to naval history and tradition, educating them in the importance of maritime forces to our nation, and explaining to them the opportunities available in maritime careers.

There are two coeducational programs: the Naval Sea Cadet Corps (NSCC) for ages fourteen to seventeen and the Navy League Cadet Corps (NLCC) for ages eleven to thirteen. There are about two hundred NSCC and NLCC units across the United States and in Puerto Rico, with more than seventy-five hundred officers and cadets involved. Sea Cadets receive their training aboard ships, planes, and at shore installations of the navy and coast guard. In addition, they are authorized to attend a two-week recruit training experience. Graduates are eligible for advanced training through special shipboard programs held during school holidays and summer months.

Programs for younger people (NLCC) do not include training aboard navy or coast guard ships or aircraft. The education covers naval history, customs and traditions, water safety, first aid, leadership procedures, and physical training. Several field trips to navy and coast guard facilities complement the lectures. Both Naval Sea Cadets and Navy League Cadets wear modified navy uniforms.

Membership in the Sea Cadets permits firsthand experience with the navy and coast guard. Cadets who decide to enlist in the navy may be eligible to do so at an advanced pay grade based on their cadet records. A scholarship fund is available for those interested in higher education. If this program appeals to you, contact the Sea Cadets group nearest to you or write the following:

Naval Sea Cadet Corps
2300 Wilson Boulevard
Arlington, VA 22201
www.seacadets.org

Sea Explorers

The exploring program of the Boy Scouts of America works for the improvement of the individual in these areas: vocation, personal fitness, citizenship, social service, and the outdoors. The Sea Explorers operate a variety of activities, some of which are listed here.

- The National Sea Explorer Sailing Championships, which is a program that originates with local councils, involves area and regional sail-offs and climaxes with national competition under the supervision of the United States Racing Union.

- Sea Explorer Rendezvous, usually held on a council, area, or regional basis, gives Explorers a chance to demonstrate through competition many of the traditional, yet practical, skills of seamanship.

- Oceanography Seminars are growing in popularity. These are usually conducted in cooperation with federal and state agencies, universities, and similar research organizations.

- Cruising is popular with Sea Explorer ships. Some cruises are held by individual ships; others involve several ships operating as a flotilla. Rivers, lakes, coastal waterways, and the open ocean are typical cruising sites. Often long-term or short-term cruises are available through the United States Navy or Coast Guard.

- High Adventure Gateways, operated by the Boy Scouts of America, are available to Sea Explorers. Of particular interest is the Florida High Adventure Gateway offering underwater exploration, skin and SCUBA diving, and sailing in the Florida Keys. The Land Between the Lakes Gateway in western Kentucky and Tennessee also offers experiences in sailing and powerboating.

- Traditional Sea Exploring centers on the sea, life and duties aboard ship, and maritime customs. In some areas this program is known as the Blue Fleet.

- Careers in Inner Space forms the basis for activities in marine sciences, fisheries, oceanography, marine architecture, and others. Persons in this program, often called the Red Fleet, frequently work with professionals in the careers they wish to enter. The exciting leisure activities of aquatics, sailing, boating, and SCUBA form a part of sea exploring; in some areas this program is known as the White Fleet.

Young adults ages fifteen to twenty-one may join Sea Exploring. Most ships are coeducational; however, some are all male, others all female. There are more than fifteen hundred Sea Explorer units with over twenty-one thousand young people involved. Many groups own their own vessels. If you wish additional information, write the following:

Sea Exploring
1325 Walnut Hill Lane
Irving, TX 75038

Naval Junior Reserve Officers Training Corps

The Naval Junior Reserve Officers Training Corps (NJROTC) offers the opportunity for secondary school students to learn about the navy, national security, and marine science and maritime topics. The curriculum runs either three or four years, depending upon the high school attended. One course is taken each year. "Naval Science III," taken during the third or fourth year, emphasizes the following concepts:

America's maritime heritage
Drills, commands, and ceremonies
Health education
Leadership
Navigation
Oceanography
Orientation of sea power

Seamanship
Shipboard indoctrination

In addition to classroom instruction, participation in the drill team (which is part of all units), the band (available at many units), and the rifle team (available at some schools) is encouraged. Those students involved in these activities engage in competitive matches with other units. Field trips and cruises form an exciting part of the program of all units. Inland units are often airlifted to coastal installations.

More than two hundred NJROTC units exist with approximately thirty thousand male and female high school students participating. Students receive one unit of credit for each year of course work. Uniforms are similar to those of active duty personnel, and the navy provides special badges and insignia. If your school has this program, contact one of the instructors for specifics. If not, you may be permitted under certain conditions to affiliate with a high school that does. Also, you may wish to work to establish a unit. Write to the navy, addressing your letter to:

NJROTC
Chief of Naval Education and Training
250 Dallas Street
Code OTE10
Pensacola, FL 32508-8520
www.njrotc.navy.mil

The Girl Scouts

Some of the finest world-of-water programs available for young people are integrated into the Girl Scouts programs for ages twelve to seventeen. Nancy Richardson, Program Specialist in Marine

Education, reports the activities resulted as a response "to those senior Girl Scouts who love the water and are eager to know more of the fascinating life of the sea and all its ramifications." The chapters, called Ships, vary widely. The Marina Scout Ship (MSS) Shangri-La in Los Altos, California, has built more than one hundred kayaks in the last several years. Based on its own success, the group has offered advice on similar programs to the Boy Scouts, 4-H, and Campfire Girls. (Some of the chapters of the latter two organizations also offer maritime and marine activities for their members; contact your local group.) Mariners also engage in ship restoration. The *Alma*, located in San Francisco, the *Adventures in Seattle*, and the *Joseph Conrad* in Mystic have benefited from their care.

Several councils offer summer opportunities in cruising. The San Jacinto group of Houston describes its trip in this way: "Long to see the world? Then 'come aboard' and experience the Texas Gulf coast as no landlubber ever has." Not to be outdone, the Toten Girl Scout Council of Seattle offers the opportunity to "hear the wind, the sails, share your dreams with a seagull, stand watch, cook in a gimballed galley, sleep at anchor, build a sand castle, and sing chanties." The Napa-Solano chapter of Vallejo, California, has organized The Trip Around the Bay. Participants "awake each morning at the California Maritime Academy to a glistening view of the Carquinez Straits—fastest flowing waters of the bay." Then they travel to different learning sites to experience the plant and animal life of the marshes and water.

Other programs—Canadian Canoe Trails, Finger Lakes Sailing Festival, Hellhole Swamp Stomp, and Spree by the Sea—offer wonderfully enjoyable and educational adventures. Girl Scouts from all over the country travel to participate in them. Most activities are open to young women only. However, some are coed and others are held in cooperation with Sea Explorers. In addition to the cruises available nationally, numerous ships and local councils for ages six to twelve engage in marine and maritime studies. For more information contact a local group (local councils are listed in the telephone book).

Career immersion in the marine and maritime specialties often involves more than wet feet!

Maritime Museums

Alabama

Dauphin Island: Fort Gaines Museum, USS *Hartford*
Gulf Shores: Fort Morgan Museum (lighthouses)
Mobile: USS *Alabama*, USS *Drum*, USS *Tecumseh*

Alaska

Juneau: Relics of USS *Juneau*

California

Dana Point: Nautical Heritage Museum
Long Beach: SS *Queen Mary*
Monterey: Allen Knight Maritime Museum, *The San Diego*
Port Hueneme: Seabee Museum
San Diego: Maritime Museum of San Diego

San Francisco: San Francisco Maritime National Historical
   Park, *C. A. Thayer* (schooner), *Gjoa* (steam-schooner)
   and others; Treasure Island Museum
San Pedro: Los Angeles Maritime Museum

Connecticut

Bridgeport: HMS *Rose*
Essex: The Connecticut River Museum, *The American
   Turtle*
Groton: Nautilus Memorial
Mystic: Marine Historical Association and Mystic Seaport,
   Charles W. Morgan (whale ship), *Joseph Conrad* (ship),
   L. S. Dunton (schooner), *Annie* (sandbagger), *Fox*
   (cutter), *Estella A.* (sloop), *Bowdoin* (schooner), *Dorothy
   Parsons*, *Regina M.*, *Pleione* (schooner), *Gundel*
New London: United States Coast Guard Museum, *The
   Eagle*

Delaware

Christiana: A number of ships under restoration
Lewes: Cannon Ball Marine Museum; University of
   Delaware Marine Science Center; *Overfalls* Maritime
   Museum
Wilmington: USCGC *Mohawk*; *Kalmar Nyckel* (recreation
   of a Swedish ship) cruises the Delaware Bay

District of Columbia

Santa Maria; Smithsonian Institution, Hall of American
   Maritime Enterprise; Navy Museum; United States

Naval Historical Display Center, Washington Navy
Yard; Washington National Archives

Florida

Fort Lauderdale: *Jungle Cruise* (paddleboat)
Key West: Mel Fisher Maritime Heritage Society
Marathon: Sunken Treasure Ship Museum
Pensacola: Naval Aviation Museum
St. Petersburg: HMS *Bounty* (restoration)

Georgia

Atlanta: HMS *Bounty* exhibit
Columbus: Confederate Naval Museum; CSS *Muscogee*,
   CSS *Chattahoochee*
Savannah: Model of SS *Savannah* at City Hall; Ships of the
   Sea Maritime Museum, *Flying Cloud* (eight-foot model),
   Harbor Queen

Hawaii

Honolulu: USS *Arizona* Memorial, Pacific Submarine
   Museum

Illinois

Chicago: Chicago Maritime Society; Museum of Science
   and Industry, *U-505* (German submarine, World War
   II); replica of Viking ship in Lincoln Park
Lockport: Illinois and Michigan Canal Museum
Peoria: *Belle Reynolds*

Indiana

Jeffersonville: Howard Steamboat Museum

Iowa

Dubuque: *Fred W. Woodward* Riverboat Museum
Keokuk: Keokuk River Museum, *George M. Verity*

Kentucky

Louisville: *Belle of Louisville*

Louisiana

Baton Rouge: Louisiana Naval War Memorial
New Orleans: CSS *Pioneer*; Louisiana State Museum

Maine

Bath: Maine Maritime Museum; *Sherman Zwicker*;
   wooden boatbuilding
Castine: Allie Ryan Maritime Museum
Portland: Lightship *Nantucket*
Searsport: Penobscot Marine Museum

Maryland

Annapolis: Historic Annapolis, Inc., Slicer Shiplap House;
   United States Naval Academy Museum; United States
   Naval Academy Library
Baltimore: Maryland Historical Society, Marine Wing;
   USS *Constellation*; the Steamship Historical Society of

America Library; Inner Harbor Baltimore Maritime
Museum; *The Chesapeake*, USS *Torsk*; Baltimore
Museum of Industry, *The Baltimore*; Calvert County
Marine Museum
Cambridge: Bannock Maritime Museum
Chesapeake City: C & D Canal Museum
Landover Hills: Nautical Research Guild
Piney Point: *Dauntless*, Harry Lundeberg Schools of
Seamanship, *Manitou*
St. Michaels: Chesapeake Bay Maritime Museum, Hooper
Strait Lighthouse

Massachusetts

Andover: Addison Gallery of American Art, Phillips
Academy
Barnstable: The Donald G. Trayser Memorial Museum
Boston: Boston Marine Society; Museum of Fine Arts; Old
State House; Museum of Science, Science Park; State
Street Trust Company; Stebbins Marine Collection,
Harrison Grey Otis House; USS *Constitution*, Boston
Tea Party Ship and Museum
Cambridge: Francis Russell Hart Nautical Museum,
Massachusetts Institute of Technology
Chatham: Whaling Museum
Cohasset: Maritime Museum
Edgartown: Dukes County Historical Society, Martha's
Vineyard
Fall River: Fall River Historical Society Museum; USS
Massachusetts, State Pier, USS *Lionship*; USS *John
Kennedy*

Gloucester: Cape Ann Historical Museum, Gloucester
Fisherman's Museum

Milton: Museum of the American China Trade

Nantucket: Nantucket Whaling Museum, Nantucket
Lifesaving Museum

New Bedford: Whaling Museum and Old Dartmouth
Historical Society

Plymouth: *Mayflower II* (replica)

Salem: Peabody Museum; Salem Maritime National
Historic Sites; Custom House; Essex Institute

Sharon: Kendall Whaling Museum

Michigan

Detroit: Detroit Historical Society; Dossin Museum of
Great Lakes History, Belle Isle

Mackinac Island: Mackinac Maritime Park

Menominee: Mystery Ship Seaport

Sault Ste. Marie: Museum ship *Valley Camp*, a Great Lakes
freighter

South Haven: Lake Michigan Maritime Museum

Minnesota

Winona: Transportation Museum on board the *Julius C.
Wilkie*

Mississippi

Biloxi: Seafood Industry Museum

Vicksburg: USS *Cairo* Museum

Missouri

Hannibal: *Mark Twain* (steamer)
Hermann: Historic Hermann Museum, including
Riverboat Room
St. Louis: Missouri Historical Society, River Room, Golden
Rod, USS *Inaugural*

Nebraska

Brownville: Museum of Missouri River History

New Hampshire

Portsmouth: Port of Portsmouth Maritime Museum,
library, paintings, ship models

New Jersey

Barnegat Light: Historical Society Museum, typical of
many of the museums located along the New Jersey
coast; Barnegat Lighthouse
Beach Haven: Long Beach Island Historical Society
Camden: USS *New Jersey* (battleship)
Hackensack: U.S. Naval Museum/Submarine, USS *Ling*
Hoboken: Hudson Waterfront Museum, the *Philip T.
Feeney* (tugboat)
Paterson: City of Paterson Museum, *Fenian Ram*
Sandyhook: Sandyhook lighthouse

New York

Amagansett: Town Marine Museum
Amsterdam: Fort Hunter, Erie Canal Locks

Brooklyn: Brooklyn Museum
Buffalo: Buffalo and Erie County Naval and Serviceman's
   Park
Clayton: Thousand Islands Shipyard Museum
Cold Spring Harbor: Vanderbilt Marine Museum
East Hampton: East Hampton Town Marine Museum
Glen Cove, Long Island: Webb Institute of Naval
   Architecture
High Falls: Delaware & Hudson Canal Museum
Huntington: Whaling Museum Society
Hyde Park: Franklin D. Roosevelt Library and Museum
Kings Point: American Merchant Marine Museum,
   National Maritime Hall of Fame
Kingston: Hudson River Maritime Center, *Mathilda*
Lake Champlain: Fort Ticonderoga Museum
New York City: India House, Hanover Square;
   Metropolitan Museum of Art; Museum of Science and
   Industry; Seamen's Church Institute; New York Public
   Library, Fifth Avenue at Forty-Second Street; South
   Street Seaport, *Ambrose* lightship, *Lettie G. Howard*,
   Alexander Hamilton; Sea-Air-Space Museum, USS
   Intrepid, USS Growler, USS *Edson*
Sag Harbor: Suffolk County Whaling Museum
Staten Island: Staten Island Museum, The Steamship
   Historical Society of America Library; National
   Lighthouse Center and Museum
Syracuse: Erie Canal Museum
West Sayville: Suffolk Marine Museum

North Carolina

Beaufort: North Carolina Maritime Museum (This museum conducts a number of programs of interest to the public and for those with an interest in marine or maritime careers.)

Kinston: CSS *Neuse*, Governor Richard Caswell Memorial

Manteo: *Elizabeth II* State Historic Site

Wilmington: USS *North Carolina* Memorial

Ohio

Canal Fulton: Canal Fulton Heritage Society Museum, *St. Helena II*

Cleveland: Great Lakes Historical Society

Fairport Harbor: Fairport Marine Museum

Marietta: Ohio River Museum, *W. P. Snyder* (steamboat)

Vermillion: Great Lakes Historical Society Museum

Oklahoma

Muskogee: Muskogee War Memorial Park and Military Museum

Oregon

Astoria: Columbia River Maritime Museum

Newport: Old Yacquina Bay Lighthouse

Portland: Oregon Historical Museum

Pennsylvania

Doylestown: Marine Room, Bucks County Historical Society

Erie: Erie Historical Museum and Planetarium

Philadelphia: Franklin Institute; Independence Seaport
Museum; Titanic Historical Society Collection, Atwater
Kent Museum; CIGNA Museum; Penn's Landing; USS
Olympia; *Welcome* (replica of William Penn's ship);
Gazela; *Mosulu*; *Barnegat*

Rhode Island

Bristol: Herreshoff Marine Museum

East Greenwich: Varnum Military and Naval Museum

Newport: Museum of Yachting, *Shamrock V*, Naval War
College Museum

Providence: Seaport '76 Foundation, *The Providence*
(replica)

South Carolina

Charleston: Patriot's Point Maritime and Naval Museum,
USS *Yorktown*, NS *Savannah*, and others

South Dakota

Sioux Falls: Battleship *South Dakota*

Tennessee

Jacksonville: USS *Key West*, USS *Tawah*, USS *Elfin*
(restoration planned)

Memphis: Mississippi River Museum at Mudd Island

Texas

Corpus Christi: USS *Lexington* Museum on the Bay
Fredericksburg: Fleet Admiral Chester W. Nimitz
    Historic Park
Galveston: *Elissa*
Rockport: Texas Maritime Museum

Vermont

Shelburne: Shelburne Museum, *Ticonderoga* (paddle-wheel
    steamer)

Virginia

Alexandria: Alexandria Seaport Foundation, Alexandria
    Waterfront Museum
Jamestown: *Discovery, Goodspeed,* and *Susan Constant*
Newport News: The Mariners Museum
Norfolk: Hampton Roads Naval Museum, USS *Franklin*
    (bridge of ship), SS *United States*
Portsmouth: Portsmouth Naval Shipyard Museum,
    Portsmouth Coast Guard Museum, *Portsmouth*
    (lightship)
Virginia Beach: Cape Henry Lighthouse, Maritime
    Historical Museum
Williamsburg: Jamestown Settlement
Yorktown: Colonial National Park Museum

Washington

Bremerton: Bremerton Naval Museum

See also the following websites for more information:

http://ils.unc.edu/maritime/home.shtml
http://www.bb62museum.org/wrldnmus.html

Recommended Reading

Books

Smith, Robert H. *Smith's Guide to Maritime Museums of North America* (3 volumes). 1st Books Library, 2002. (See also www.maritimemuseums.net.)

Stanford, Joseph. *Sea History's Guide to American and Canadian Maritime Museums*. Peekskill, NY: National Maritime Historical Society, 1990.

Periodicals

American Neptune
Peabody Museum
East India Square
Salem, MA 01970

An academic research publication of the Salem Peabody Museum. Contains interesting articles of a scholarly nature and provides excellent information on America's maritime history.

Blue Planet
The Ocean Conservancy
1725 De Sales St. NW, Ste. 600
Washington, DC 20036
A magazine with a strong commitment to the preservation of marine life and the planet.

Boating
1633 Broadway, 43rd Fl.
New York, NY 10009
A popular, nicely illustrated magazine containing historical, contemporary, and how-to articles. Students will find advertisements as well as articles of interest.

Cruising World
Sailing Company
Box 3400
Newport, RI 02840
A popular magazine aimed at readers interested in sailing. Each issue contains articles on technique, possible adventures, tours, and other general sailing–related topics. Students will enjoy the illustrations and advertisements.

Current: The Journal of Marine Educators
National Marine Educators Association
P.O. Box 1470
Ocean Springs, MS 39566-1470
This well-written periodical contains popular articles as well as updates of marine science and maritime affairs.

Dolphin Log
870 Greenbrier Circle, Ste. 402
Chesapeake, VA 23320

A well-written marine science–oriented publication from the Cousteau Society for younger children.

The Log of Mystic Seaport
Mystic Seaport
Mystic, CT 06355
A well-done research-oriented publication whose focus is on maritime history.

Marine Conservation News
Center for Marine Conservation
1725 DeSales St. NW
Washington, DC 20036
A newsletter filled with updates on all aspects of marine life.

Marine Mammal Science
Dr. Glen Van Blaricom School of Fisheries
University of Washington
Seattle, WA 98195
A publication for those with a strong interest in this field.

Naval History
U.S. Naval Institute Circulation Department
2062 Generals Hwy.
Annapolis, MD 21401
An excellent publication that covers popular history, research, and some less-known aspects of naval history.

Nor'Easter
A publication that contains updates on research related to the sea as well as updates on northeast regional programs. Each of the Sea Grant colleges regularly publishes such a journal. Contact your regional college (see Chapter 3) for a subscription.

Oceanus
Woods Hole Oceanographic Institute
360 Woods Hole Rd.
Woods Hole, MA 02543
A quarterly publication investigating and reporting recent findings on the sea. Topics also cover the frontiers of sea research.

Professional Mariner
Navigator Publishing
18 Danforth St.
Portland, ME 04101
Published six times a year, this magazine focuses upon navigation and seamanship.

Propeller Club Quarterly
3927 Old Lee Hwy., No.101A
Fairfax, VA 22030
Provides the reader with current happenings in the U.S. maritime community from shipping to port security.

SCUBA Diving
Rodale Press
33 E. Minor St.
Emmaus, PA 18098
A lavishly illustrated monthly magazine focusing upon all aspects of scuba from equipment to interesting dives.

Sea Heritage News
Sea Heritage Foundation
254-26 Seventy-Fifth St.
Glen Oaks, NY 11004

A newspaper with a wide variety of maritime-humanities articles (art, language, history).

Sea History
National Maritime Historical Society
5 John Walsh Blvd.
Box 68
Peekskill, NY 10566
Each issue of this fine periodical contains historical articles as well as current issues of a historical and humanities interest. Additionally, maritime art receives attention.

Sea Horse
NJ MEA
c/o Bruce Boyd
MAST Science Department
Sandy Hook, NJ 07732
This quarterly newsletter of the New Jersey Marine Education Association provides an insight to a variety of marine science/education activities.

Sea Power
Navy League
2300 Wilson Blvd.
Arlington, VA 22201
An independent, nonprofit, civilian education organization. Recent editions have contained illustrated articles on various aspects of the maritime life-fishing industry, oceanography, and shipbuilding.

Steamboat Bill
300 Ray Dr., Ste. 4
Providence, RI 02906

This quarterly publication of the Steamship Historical Society of America contains short, interesting, well-illustrated features on topics such as ferryboats, Mississippi showboats, and other non-naval steamships.

U.S. Naval Institute Proceedings
U.S. Naval Institute
2062 Generals Highway
Annapolis, MD 21402
A publication of the United States Naval Institute, a private, professional society for all who are interested in naval and maritime affairs. Past issues of this more than 125-year-old journal constitute an excellent source of maritime (especially naval) history. More recent issues deal with contemporary maritime and naval problems. The institute also publishes books related to naval and maritime affairs.

Wooden Boat
Wooden Boat
Box 78
Brooklin, ME 04616
A bimonthly magazine on present-day building, repair, and restoration of wooden craft.

ABOUT THE AUTHOR

RAY HEITZMANN, PH.D., a faculty member at Villanova University, has a national reputation in the area of marine and maritime studies. His articles on these topics have appeared in *Sea World, Shipmate, Sea History, Sea Heritage News, The U.S. Naval Institute Proceedings, The Beachcomber,* the *Journal of Marine Education, Naval History, Long Beach Island Magazine, American Neptune,* and others. He also has run career education workshops and courses and has published related articles in *Career World, Real World,* and the *California Social Studies Review.* For several years he authored a column in *Long Beach Island Magazine* entitled "Nautically Notable and the World of Water."

Heitzmann has served as a high school teacher and as a basketball coach in Illinois, New York, and Pennsylvania; he is also the former head men's basketball coach at Neumann College in Pennsylvania. Following undergraduate work at Villanova University, he received his master's degree from the University of Chicago and his

Ph.D. from the University of Delaware. He has taken additional graduate studies at California State University at San Jose and Northwestern University in Illinois.

Heitzmann has been selected for inclusion in *Who's Who in America*, *Who's Who in Education*, *Contemporary Authors*, and other volumes. A frequent speaker at conferences, schools, and aquaria, he has a strong commitment to reminding Americans of not only our nation's nautical heritage, but also the importance and value of the marine environment.